Exploring the smaller Towns of Somerset

Geoffrey Body

All good wishes
Geoff Body

KINGSMEAD PRESS

KINGSMEAD PRESS
ISBN 1 85026 017 6

Published 2000 by Kingsmead Press
74 Ryder Street, Pontcanna, Cardiff CF11 9BU
Printed by J & P Davison
3 James Place, Treforest, Pontypridd CF37 1SQ
Copyright Geoffrey Body and Kingsmead Press

Exploring *the smaller* Towns of Somerset

Introduction, Use and Acknowledgements

The idea for this book arose from the writer's own visits to the smaller towns of Somerset where there seemed to be so much of interest to see but sadly no readily available guide to help in understanding it. The solution lay in using the wide variety of sources from libraries, museums and information offices and especially from the extensive facilities provided by the Somerset Studies Library at Taunton to which I owe a special debt of gratitude. The value of this research was revealed in how often my own town visit had missed something which would have been of special interest if only I had known about it.

This book attempts to deal with this situation by offering information on the origins and nature of each town and by devising a walk that will encompass the major features of interest. It also provides a gazetteer of such features in each of the main streets, which are recorded in walk order. In addition to the other illustrations a simple street map is provided with each entry and bears location numbers which correspond with those used in the text.

With little to define *town* or *small* the choice of entries for inclusion has inevitably been a matter of personal choice. It does not pretend to be comprehensive and there are many other larger villages and towns with their own high interest. Perhaps they may feature in a future volume but meantime the responsibility for the choice is mine.

Similarly while every effort has been made to achieve accuracy, some information is just not available; in other cases sources do not always agree and, of course, the passage of time inevitably produces change. Although no responsiblilty can be accepted for the contents of this book, we would like to know of any detail in which readers believe it to be incorrect.

My companion in the process of exploration and research has been my good friend Roy Gallop who has contributed greatly to the process of preparing this work, not least in providing the line drawings used. I also need to thank my publishers for their faith in the project and my wife for her patient checking to ensure that left turn does mean left and that the number quoted in text against the church is not really the old bakery. Special thanks go to Jim Noble who guided much of the production and, to many others who have contributed information so willingly, please accept this as grateful recognition.

AXBRIDGE

HISTORY

Axbridge is a town of great charm, its rich history apparent the moment you arrive and its streets and buildings full of high interest. Many date partly from medieval times and were the homes of prosperous merchants, built close together in a long, narrow profile and much modified subsequently. Later centuries added their own houses and style variations to create an intriguing but entirely pleasing mixture.

The Moorland Street car park is located roughly in the middle of the original Saxon burh and The Square nearby still has a flavour of the medieval period, supported by the fine Somerset Perpendicular church, 15th century wells and some notable timberframed buildings dating back to the 1500s. In later years the market cross and stocks stood here and each November a bull was loosed and then hounded along High Steet to a death that provided meat for the poor.

Standing between the Mendip hills and the Axe and Yeo rivers, Axbridge was originally one of the fortified Saxon sites around the royal palace at Cheddar. By the end of the 10th century it had its own market, 32 burgesses and a mint, and under later Norman rule developed as a centre for royal hunting activity. King John granted Axbridge a charter around 1204 and other charters followed confirming the town's right to hold a market, its 1557 borough status and the four annual fairs around which much of the commercial activity of the community was centred.

Drawing its supplies from Mendip sheep, Axbridge was an important wool town for many years with a number of Hugenots settling there and a growing reputation for knitted stockings. The land around is fertile and agriculture has grown steadily in importance over the centuries, helped by the coming of the railway in 1869.

Agriculture still makes a significant contribution to the economy of the area and tourism is also important. The town museum is housed in King John's Hunting Lodge and facilities exist for sailing on the reservoir outside the town.

The Old Drugstore (left) and King John's Hunting Lodge (right) give this end of Axbridge High Street a medieval look. Only the modern road sign spoils the illusion.

THE WALK

Park off and then explore Moorland Street. Walk around and savour The Square. Exit via St Mary's Street, passing along the south side and returning on the north. Take the lane opposite The Court House and pass round the church to regain The Square by the wells. Exit along High Street and West Street, turning left at the end of the town and back to the starting point via Houlgate Way.

GAZETTEER

Moorland Street - This was once the main street through the Saxon burh and a road that led to the royal palace at Cheddar. It now leads only to the moor but has some pleasant and varied buildings including The Old Almshouse (1) which was built in 1475 and served the poor of the town until the Axbridge Union Workhouse was opened. The interior of the building opposite is of a similar age.

The Square - The eye is caught first by the 3-storey, timber framed building on the corner of High Street. Known as King John's Hunting Lodge (2) this is a misnomer for the building originated around 1500, possibly as a merchant's house. It certainly served as a group of shops and alehouse for a while; now it is the town museum.

To the east of Moorland Street is the 1830 town hall (3) and on its roof the alarm bell that used to bring the old fire pump into action. The ground floor was used as a market hall with the town's civic functions administered above. On the opposite corner to the town hall the 1830s Lamb Inn (4) stands on the site of the former Guild Hall. The building of the Town Hall ended civic meetings there and the markets in the nearby Shambles which had replaced the 14th century market cross around 1756.

All the buildings around The Square hold great interest and many that have been refronted still have

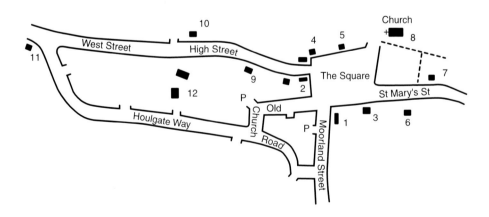

6

medieval interior features. The north side includes The Old Angel (5), a former inn dating back to around 1550, a slightly later shop/house once used by the Somerset Co-operative Society and the attractive Lloyds Bank House.

St Mary's Street - Another area of great variety with many of the houses having Georgian styling or features. Of special note are The Court House of 1796 (6) and The Old Court House (7) which, with Stanley House, is a c1800 rebuild of a much earlier structure, also Park House, Brooks House, The Georgian House and others.

The Church - The parish church of St John the Baptist (8) with its fine roof and elaborate tower dates back to around 1400 but was extensively restored in 1888 by J.D. Sedding. There are numerous memorials to local worthies and such curiosities as the *caged* tomb in the churchyard remembering Helier Garbet Jeune. The nearby church rooms started life as two 15th century cottages.

By the side of the church approach steps are twin wells surmounted by medieval arches and rare examples of the survival of a town's public water supply for 500 years. A plaque describes their origins as a hill-fed reservoir for a former water mill located just to the west.

High Street - Nowhere is the medieval face of Axbridge more apparent than at the start of this narrow main street. The National Trust building on the corner is followed by two more 16th century buildings with jettied upper storeys on the left (No. 9 The Butcher's Shop which has an ornate doorway and the less dramatic No. 15 St Judes) and another, The Old Drugstore (Nos. 4 and 5), on the right. They all repay study as do the 17th century buildings which follow. No. 19 The Old Manor House (9) was refronted in 1804 and is notable for its ornate cupola and 1752 weather vane on top. The Bank House (10) further up on the right is also of interest.

West Street - This continuation of High Street maintains the architectural interest of Axbridge. Most of the houses are late 18th or early 19th century (as the Methodist church is) although Nos. 22, 24, 44 and 50 date from the 17th. At the end is Compton House (11), the former 17th century manor house home of the Prowse family, much in evidence in the church.

St John's Court - From West Street and the return walk route down Houlgate Way it is possible to see parts of the Union Workhouse complex (12) which brought status and employment to Axbridge when it opened in 1837. It consists of a hospital building and the main workhouse building now converted to residential use. Note the pretentious frontage and the plainer former dormitory area in red conglomerate behind.

BRUTON

HISTORY

Bruton has mercifully escaped random development and can still offer a variety and charm that derives from a venerable history. Its origins go back to late Saxon times when Bruton was one of Somerset's several royal boroughs, centred around a ford across the River Brue and important enough to have its own mint. It grew in stature in the Norman era when an Augustinian priory was established sometime around 1130.

Recent research suggests some Bruton buildings may have features dating back to the 12th century. Certainly there is much evidence of the long wool trade years which produced the wealth to replace the ancient church, convert the priory to a full-blown abbey, establish a famous school and endow the almshouses. The pasturing of sheep and processing of their wool was to dominate Bruton until well into the 1700s when northern competition brought a change to silk working and the conversion of the town's several mills. By this time the abbey had been *dissolved*, a fine house built on the site for the Berkeley family and then burned down in 1763 and the church had gained a second 15th century tower to add to its smaller 14th century one.

Signs in the churchyard and in Patwell Street mark past flood levels and give a major clue to the basic layout of Bruton where the High Street runs parallel to the modest Brue but at a higher level. It is a street of incredible interest from which alleys, such as the 16th century Amor Barton, run down to the level of a former mill stream and the river beyond. Across the ford, now marked by stepping stones, or the packhorse bridge which led to the abbey, lies a street curiously named Plox which has a surviving part of the abbey wall on one side and a variety of old buildings, some part of King's School, on the other. At the east end of town Quaperlake Street offers further period variety while the later West End has a number of mill buildings which were powered either from the river or an artificial mill pond on the slope above.

After the decline in the silk trade Bruton surrendered its specialisation for a more cosmopolitan profile with a mixture of country industries, lace, horsehair for furniture, brewing, bacon curing and so on. Happily its configuration did not welcome traffic or major rebuilding and today's visitors derive a considerable benefit from the absence of major change in the centre of this historic and picturesque town.

THE WALK

Bruton can be reached by train, bus or car and a convenient place to begin the walk is at the bridge opposite the church. Climb Patwell Street to the junction with High Street but explore the beginnings of Quaperlake Street right and Coombe Street ahead.

Return to the junction and savour the rich variety of High Street. At the end is West End which is also worth wandering around before crossing Legg Bridge and taking the footpath (L) beyond to cut the corner to Plox. Down Plox turning left over the Packhorse Bridge and right along a footpath will lead back to the church starting point.

The wall along the curiously-named Plox at Bruton was once part of the abbey boundary. The 1822 vicarage stands behind.

GAZETTEER

Patwell Street - This is the area of the old Saxon town, starting with the bridge (1) which dates from 1757 but was widened in 1835. At one corner an 18th century pumphouse stands on the site of St Patrick's Well. The winding street itself then leads up via varied period houses to Nos.3 and 5 (2), once Bruton's main coaching inn, the Old Bull. A plaque on the left marks the flood level of June 28th 1917.

Quaperlake Street - The pleasant library building on the corner is followed by late 18th/early 19th century houses in local stone rubble. Next the 17th century Glen House was first the home of a silk throwster and then, from 1889, housed Sexey's School until its own building was ready. The Viney's Yard area (3) beyond was associated with fulling, silk, horsehair, bacon products and transport before becoming a residential development. On the left hand side note Quaperlake House and its companions.

Coombe Street - The Blue Ball of 1765-70 (4) was once the White Hart Inn and embraces fine Georgian assembly rooms, stables and coach-house. Another coach-house opposite dates from 1780 and is followed by the St David's Place area, once home of the town's artisans and the excise officer.

High Street - The street and its *bartons* have a medieval layout and not a few interior remnants of that period. Virtually every building (5) is of interest starting with No.1, once part of the White Hart and then an ironmonger's from 1798. Next on the right is the delightful pharmacy, once the *gentleman's house* of John Dampier. Nos. 5 and 7 were the 1577 George Inn, No. 13 has medieval cellars and No. 29 was once a branch of Stuckey's Bank.

In the first part of the street on the left Nos.18 and 20 date back to the 16th century while No.28 (6) was an inn, allegedly with hidden passages for avoiding the Excise men, before rebuilding in 1768 as a house and silk mill, conversion in 1803 to a chapel and the start of a new life in 1997. Next door are the Priory House and the late 15th century Priory Court House, jettied, decorated and dormered.

Back to the north side of the street for the Masonic Hall group of buildings (7) dating from 1642 and used as the Market Hall Court House until 1790. No. 45 is the 18th century Castle Inn on the site of the old White Ball Inn. There are weavers'cottages up St Catherine's Hill while further on are the Silk Mill group (8) and No. 91 which belonged to Hugh Sexey, founder of Sexey's Hospital (9) on the other side of the street. This was rebuilt from old charity houses after Sexey's death in 1619, housing the elderly poor and the first youngsters of what was in 1891 to become Sexey's School. No. 72, the 17th century Old Brewery House, was once part of the hospital.

West End - This end of the High Street has The Square, an 1897 chapel (now the Bruton Centre) and Mill Lane (10),

where No.8 was one of Bruton's three grist mills.

Opposite a footpath leads to the mill pond and right, up West End proper, are more mill buildings, the Methodist Church and Turnpike Cottage (11).

Plox - The upper Kings School group includes the Memorial Hall (12) right and the Headmaster's House and tower (13) left. Below are St Mary's Vicarage (14) built against the abbey wall in 1822, and opposite, the 1520 original Old House group and the 1687 Plox House (15). The parallel river is crossed by the 15th century packhorse bridge (16).

The Church - A 13th century crypt lies below the classical 1743 chancel in this fine Somerset church (17) with its twin towers and standing below the dovecote on the hill.

CASTLE CARY

HISTORY

Many of Castle Cary's buildings are in mellow local hamstone, giving the town a warm, welcoming look. It is a pleasant and historic place and something of that history can be visualised by walking up Paddock Drain to gaze upwards to the Iron Age fort on the skyline and then down over the undulating ground where once stood a sizeable castle and the manor house that succeeded it. The Norman castle was besieged in 1138 in the on-going dispute between Stephen and the barons favouring Matilda. Famine forced its surrender but it was back in the conflict again in 1148 and later fell into decay, its Lovel owners moving to the adjacent manor house.

From Tudor times onwards Castle Cary added quality woollens to its agricultural activity, first as a cottage

industry and then in water-powered mills along the Cary River. One of the town's four annual fairs was devoted to the cloth makers who represented a significant proportion of the population and produced much of its wealth. After the trade was lost to the north at the end of the 17th century the emphasis changed to the manufacture of rope, twine, webbing and sailcloth and making use of the flax crop grown locally. The Donne family pioneered this activity at nearby Ansford in 1797 and built the Higher Flax Mills in Torbay Road, Castle Cary to house it from 1818.

In 1837 John Boyd set up his horse-hair business in modest premises in Chapel Yard, moving to buildings in the old sheep market area in 1851. As John Boyd Textiles the activity has survived in a specialised form using horsehair from China. After a troubled genesis the railway finally reached Castle Cary in 1856, the station in Ansford later becoming part of the West of England main line. In recent years the town's business activity has embraced milk, crate manufacture, timber, tyre remoulds, veterinary supplies, electrical goods and until 1991, Clark's shoes.

Today Castle Cary retains much evidence of its rich and varied past but also presents a pleasant modern face. In their warm Cary stone its buildings vary from tiny cottages and the 7ft diameter lock-up to the venerable church and the houses and mills of a past merchant society.

In the centre of Castle Cary is this fine market house building. An excellent museum is housed in what were once the upper reading and entertainment rooms.

THE WALK

Start near the horsepond and explore Park Street, Church Street and then South Street as far as Chapel Yard. Return and turn left at the Triangle, right into Woodcock Street and then left up Bailey Hill and Florida Street. Returning take further lefts to gain High Street and Upper High Street. Return again as far as Fore Street with a deviation up Paddock Drain left before continuing ahead to the starting point.

GAZETTEER

Park Street - Near to Park Pond, the source of the River Cary, the Primary School (1) dates from 1840 and was formerly a National School, extended in 1876. Note the former fire engine house nearby. Beyond, on a medieval site, is Manor Farm House (2) which dates from around 1600.

Church Street - The Church of All Saints (3) has Saxon origins although today's building dates from c1470 with a mid-19th century rebuild which added a spire to the basic Perpendicular style. The church has several chest tombs and an 1846 vicarage.

South Street - Scotland House was once a private school. Belle Vue and Ferndale villas and South Cottage all date back to the 17th century. Centaur House of 1865 was the site of Mathews factory from 1815.

Chapel Yard - The houses on the left (4) are where John Boyd started horse hair weaving in 1837. Opposite is the nicely refurbished Congregational Chapel (5) built in 1815 on the site of the old Golden Lion Inn.

Woodcock Street - A varied collection of houses from the 17-19th centuries. Beyond Priory Close was Florida House built in 1818 and taking its name from a local 1768 expedition to Florida. T.S. Donne purchased the site in 1881 and built the present towered edifice (6) which later became St John's Priory.

Bailey Hill - On the left are a former horsehair factory and ropewalk (7). Opposite is the pleasant 1767 Post Office (8) and between them the Round House, a small former lock-up building 10ft high, 7ft in diameter and constructed of Keinton Mandeville stone. A plaque records its building in

1779 for £23 derived from two 16th century bequests to the poor.

Florida Street - Leading to the old Mathews factory there is, on the left (9), a c1714 cottage, the Old School Room, the Old Armoury and the wall of a former ropewalk.

Market Place - The 1855 Market House (10) by F.C. Penrose for the Market House Company replaced a 1616 predecessor in the expectation of business from the railway. Reading and social rooms were provided above the lower corn market and lock-up area and the building now houses a fine museum and information activities. Opposite, the George Hotel (11) dates from the 1600s or even earlier and incorporates some former castle stonework.

(Upper) High Street - Starting with the ornate 1826 bank building on the left (12), the interest and variety continues all the way up to North Street. The house on the corner of Ansford Road has associations with Parson Woodforde and John Wesley and the Ochil Tree House group (13) of c1825 was part of the Boyd empire, acting as home and offices from 1851. Douglas MacMillan MBE, the great contributor to cancer relief, also lived there. Opposite is the c1840 Wesleyan Methodist Church (14).

Fore Street - White & Sons building dates from 1804 and a milepost from the Wightman Foundry from around the same date. The horsepond (15), with the war memorial in the centre, is fed from Park Pond. An open stream used to run down Fore Street and skins were washed in the stretch between the horsepond and Skin House where the green skins were inspected on behalf of the Court Leet.

A visit should also made to Torbay Road to see the High Flax Mills complex - former ropewalk, entrance lodge and three mills.

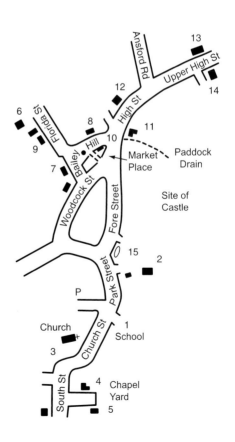

CHEDDAR

HISTORY

For up to 100,000 years man has inhabited the low terrace on which modern Cheddar is located, a fertile, sheltered spot where the Mendip hills rise from the coastal plain. Our early ancestors left their tools and their bones in the caves to which visitors now flock each summer, filling the lower reaches of the dramatic Cheddar Gorge with all the life and colour that tourists bring to an area. Nearby is another, calmer Cheddar with much to show of its varied past and prepared richly to reward a little study and imagination.

Cheddar had a small Roman presence and was a substantial royal lodge-cum-palace in Saxon times, the complex including successive great halls, mills, domestic buildings and the meeting room used at least three times by the Witan assembly in the 10th century. One of Somerset's five forests, Cheddar's royal hunting tradition continued under Norman rule but after King John's rebuilding of the royal apartments in 1209-11 the property later passed into the hands of Wells Cathedral.

Early medieval Cheddar gave way to the manorial years, dominated by the church and such powerful families as the de Cheddres, the Berkeleys and later the Thynnes. Drainage of the moor below increased agricultural prosperity with corn mills along the River Yeo later joined by cloth and paper mills. Cheddar cheese originated at the beginning of this period, was well known by the 16th century and had become one of the greatest cheeses in the country by the end of the 18th. Now it has been joined in importance by the strawberry crop which led to the Cheddar Valley & Yatton Railway, opened in 1869-70, becoming known as the Strawberry Line.

The first stalactite caves were discovered at Cheddar in 1837 and led to the growth of a tourist industry which helped to end the poverty and illiteracy that philanthropist Hannah More had set out to tackle in 1789. The rocks of Cheddar Gorge are home to the unique Cheddar Pink and a rare hawkweed. They also give birth to the River Yeo which follows a pleasant, winding route through the twin gorge and town settlements and helps to make up the fascinating mixture that is Cheddar.

THE WALK

Park off Church Street and explore the church area and Froglands Lane. Head for the market cross and then take two rights and a left to pick up St Andrews Road. At the end take an optional excursion up the gorge or go left across the bridge and right up Birch Hill. Turn left along Silver Street, take a look at Kent Street and then descend first Upper and then Lower North Street. Cross Station Road and return via the footpath on the left of the Kings of Wessex School and back to Church Street via Parsons Pen.

GAZETTEER

Church Street - At the market cross end the mid-18th century Court House (1) stands opposite some houses with fine decorative ironwork. Further down pleasant cottages are faced by the impressive frontage of Cheddar Church House (2). The 15th century Church Farm House (3) lies beyond the church itself.

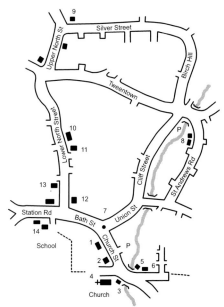

The Church - The parish church of St Andrew (4), with its delightful frontage and 110ft tower, stands on an early Roman site. It was built between 1350 and 1450, with extensive restoration by William Butterfield in 1873, and is probably the fourth church to stand here. Among the interior features is a superb carved stone pulpit from the 15th century.

Froglands Lane - An atmospheric byway with the 17th century Fairlands House (5) on the riverside corner site once occupied by a mill. Two cottages of the same period

follow (6) and behind these two former barns converted to housing. One used to be a tannery drying shed with a bark-grinding stone in the floor and a ramp for hauling skins from the water. A set of substantial ex-farm buildings on the right of the footpath has some intriguing features.

Market Cross - Reputed to be a 15th century preaching cross (7) adapted for market use. The surround was added much later with further restoration work in 1887.

St Andrews Road - A surprise in this road of pleasant modern housing is the former manor house (8) on the left, now converted to three dwellings. Nearby is a former mill, one of fifteen along the Yeo in Cheddar.

Although much altered in later years, Cheddar's market cross has 15th century origins.

15

Cheddar Gorge - On the right shops and buildings tucked up against the cliff are followed by the cave entrances. On the left there is a back route along the river with some period buildings, gardens and pleasant views of the lake.

Birch Hill - Offers a delightful variety of houses on the left side and a vantage point for looking down on the gorge approaches on the right.

Silver Street - A long, mixed street with No.1 a thatched inn (9) dating back to 1650. Neighbouring Kent Street typifies the older part of Cheddar.

Lower North Street - A very mixed and interesting thoroughfare. The 1834 National School building (10) has now been turned into homes but retains its tablet marking 42 years service by Dr W. Statham, while Hannah More's cottage (11) - which is basically

17th century with later additions - records the fact that the "author and philanthropist opened day and Sunday schools" here in 1789. The street has other 17th century buildings, a Gothic villa-cottage built for the Marquess of Bath around 1830 (Fern Bank (12) at the Station Road end) and the 1831 Baptist Chapel (13).

Station Road - Nos.1 and 2 started life as a 17th century farmhouse and some of the station buildings survive beyond the war memorial.

Kings of Wessex School - In the grounds stands a ruin on the site of what was once the chapel of the Saxon palace (14), dedicated to St Columbanus and including some very ancient stonework in its fabric. Marked out on the ground are the sites of the Great Halls, the Witan building, the corn mills and the domestic buildings.

Also of interest in Cheddar are the 1897 Methodist Church in Cliff Street, early 19th century cottages along The Cliffs and Brock Farmhouse in Hannay Road which goes back to the 16th century.

At the foot of the Cheddar Gorge the infant Yeo river, which once powered the town's water mills, now makes a pleasing water feature for its visitors.

CREWKERNE

HISTORY

Crewkerne's gracious past co-exists well with a thriving present. Not that this was always so for the centuries of prosperity derived from wool and flax were followed by leaner times which continued well into this century. However, this at least preserved the fine buildings of the 18th and 19th centuries from the developers and helped to secure for much of the present town centre well deserved classification as an area of outstanding architectural and historic interest.

A Roman road ran through Crewkerne but the settlement seems to have achieved greater prominence under Saxon rule when it was a royal estate mentioned in Alfred's will and later given a mint. The Danes ravaged the town in AD1015 but matters improved under Norman rule with much market and church activity. By the time the manor passed to the Duke of Clarence around 1463 Crewkerne was already noted for its woollens and the work of its goldsmiths.

By the 16th century Crewkerne was important as a meeting place of the Exeter road and routes to the Dorset coast. Its agriculture began to break free from tradition by growing flax to feed outworkers and small factories making a range of products from sailcloth to rope, bags and twine. The George and the White Hart were among the coaching inns which sprang up to cater for a growing number of travellers.

In 1789 the era of the larger factory arrived in Crewkerne with the building of the Sparks premises on a Parrett tributary at Viney Bridge. Works housing was provided nearby in South Street. Textile specialities included webbing, sailcloth and clothing, Crewkerne making sails for HMS Victory and serge for the East India Company. After a steady rise in population in the first half of the century, the town began to benefit from the new railway to London in 1860 with a major increase in clothing manufacture following. These years of prosperity resulted in the building of numerous Late Georgian and Regency style houses for Crewkerne's merchants.

Competition from northern looms then brought a decline in Crewkerne's affairs which it took a long time to reverse. However, the town has made great strides since the building of the first trading estate in 1958 adding three major housing developments, two shopping centres, a modern library and day centre.

THE WALK

From the South Street car park exit to Market Street and turn left and left again to explore South Street. Return and explore Hermitage Street before heading along West Street as far as Court Barton. Turn right and continue ahead, pass left around the church and down Abbey Street to the

17

Market Square. Explore East Street and Church Street and then return via Market Street to the starting point.

GAZETTEER

Market Street - This was part of the 18th century expansion of Crewkerne and many of the shops still show signs of their origins as Georgian houses. On the west side of particular note are the substantial 3-storey 1838 classical facade of the 1810 NatWest bank (1) with the building of the former Red Lion coaching inn nearby. On the opposite side No.17 (2) was the home of the Blake family on whose land the Falkland Square shopping precinct was built. Behind are the library (3) and day centre.

South Street - On the left is the tiny, elaborate, 1933 Masonic Hall (4) and

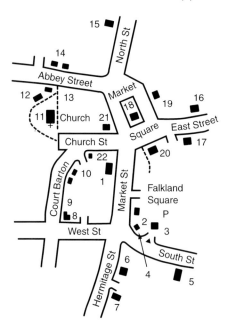

on the right the 17th century No.20 with its stone mullioned windows. Next door note The Elms and then the former Christ Church (5) built in 1852-4 in Gothic Revival style. Note too the rows of workers' cottages on the left.

Hermitage Street - On the left is the Unitarian Schoolroom and Chapel (6), an early nonconformist site dating back to 1733. A 3-storey stone house The Hermitage (7) on the corner of Pulman's Lane, was once the home of local writer and historian G.P.R. Pulman. Opposite right is Hermitage Terrace of 1879.

West Street - Chubb's Almshouses (8) occupy a corner block on the right, the West Street group dating from 1897 and a bequest by surgeon George Slade Joliffe.

Court Barton - On the corner is the original almshouse group (9), founded in 1604 by Matthew and Margaret Chubb and restored by public subscription in 1887. Further on left *Jubilee Cottage* is followed by two 1893 buildings (10) *Ye Shelle House* with protruding centre section and a smaller house with ornate window coping. Court Barton was once the site of the Courtenay's manor house.

The Church - On the site of the Saxon minster and its Norman successor, the present parish church of St Bartholomew (11) was funded by the wool-based prosperity of the 15th and 16th centuries. In style it is late Gothic

18

perpendicular with a typical 80ft Somerset tower.

Abbey Street - Abbey House (12) dates from 1846 but retains a window from one of the three medieval clergy houses formerly on the site. There is an outlet for Pople's Well on the side of the coachhouse. Between the two the Church Hall (13) was once the Old Grammar School (1499-1883) comprising schoolroom and schoolmaster's house. Opposite are some substantial 19th century villas (14) starting with No.26, built in 1828 as a school house, and St Martin's School.

North Street - On the left is the 1820 Baptist Church and manse (15). Several houses in the Nos. 62-86 group are probably 17th century.

East Street - East Street has a delightful mixture of Georgian gentry houses starting with No.2 and then Richmond House and Merefield House (16), said to be built by Robert Merefield in 1589 with additional 1661 and 1679 dates displayed and a 1810 Greek doorway. On the south side are the White Hart Hotel (17) first mentioned in 1499, the late medieval Candle Cottage, Nos. 16, 18 and 20 from the 17th century and No. 40 Townsend House, also 1600s but modified in 1733.

Market Square - The centrepiece is the elaborate Victoria Hall (18), built as a market house around 1730 and substantially rebuilt in 1900. It now serves as town hall, meeting venue and information centre. To the rear is

the Kings Arms of the early 19th century with a pleasant mix of Georgian and Victorian buildings descending the west side of the square. Note also the 1810 Cornhill House (19) and opposite, the George Hotel (20), an 1832 rebuild of a 1541 coaching inn and now giving access to a pleasant little shopping centre. Nearby are the attractive Lloyds Bank building and a dramatic 4-storey edifice with huge dormers.

Incorporating some of the features of its 1730 predecessor, Crewekerne's ornate town hall also serves as a community office and information point.

Church Street - Here is a fine mixture of Georgian houses, Nos. 6 and 8 dating from the late 17th/early 18th century and the remainder from the following 100 years. Note especially the Swan Hotel (21), bottom right and once the starting point of the London wagon, and the council office and museum group (22) top left.

Wooded slopes form a backdrop for almost every street in Dulverton, as they do in this view of High Street.

These stepping stones across the river at Bruton may have been one of the old routes between town and abbey.

Athough much restored in the 19th century this attractive timbered building in Church Street at Dunster has late medieval origins.

20

DULVERTON

HISTORY

The small town of Dulverton lies amid the beautiful vales and rivers of Exmoor with the Brendon Hills nearby. Its buildings of light grey local stone contrast with the green fields and rippling streams in summer and in the hardest of winters can represent the warmth of human activity surrounded by fields white with snow. Throughout its existence Dulverton has reflected the pastoral character of the area in which it stands, a town in which to weave and market the wool of countless Exmoor sheep or to grind the corn of the small local farms. Today it has additional facilities to serve the many tourists who delight in the shallow, hurrying rivers and rolling countryside which surround the town.

Dulverton's early history is that of a small, agricultural settlement first owned by Saxon Earl Harold and then by Norman William. A succession of Norman knights and gentry then held the manor which paid its tithes to the priory at Taunton but received little in return. The embryo township started to grow and in 1306 received a charter for a market and 3-day fair but a period of decline set in later and led to a report that the town was "in great ruin and decay". A new charter granted by Queen Mary in 1555 helped to reverse this, its trading profits being directed to the benefit of the Dulverton townspeople. The first reference to a church occurred in 1150 and medieval

Dulverton seems to have developed around the market area that sloped down from the rising ground on which the church stands to the bridge over the River Barle below.

By the 18th century Dulverton had an extensive trade in coarse woollen cloth and blankets purchased locally or carried to the more populous coastal plain by packhorse and later over the roads of the Minehead United Turnpike Trust. Still with two main streets down to the river Dulverton had several mills along the leat that cut through the town from north to south plus a brick market house and butchers' shambles.

The majority of Dulverton's present buildings date from the 19th century and include the Union workhouse built in 1855 and now the administrative centre of the Exmoor National Park. The arrival of the railway in 1873 brought increasing numbers of sportsmen to the area, increasing the demand for transport, accommodation and other local facilities. They were the forerunners of today's holiday visitors who are well catered for by this busy and interesting town, well blessed with modern facilities but still having four surviving mill buildings to act as reminders of the former wool, corn, crepe and paper industries and the 5-arch bridge over the River Barle to mark the original reason for the town's location.

THE WALK

From the car park at Barle Bridge ascend Bridge Street and turn left into Fore Street.

Explore Lady Street left and return to head along Bank Square, up the footpath by the church and on to Town Marsh before bearing right to Vicarage Hill. There turn right again and descend High Street, exploring Chapel Street at the end left before returning to the car park.

GAZETTEER

Barle Bridge - Of medieval origin, the bridge (1) was "repaired in the Yeare of our Lord God 1684" and widened in 1819. It suffered flood damage in 1866 and 1952-3. Exmoor House (2) was formerly the union workhouse built in 1855 for £4000 and housing over 50 paupers. The building had later periods as a hostel, a hospital and council offices before becoming the Exmoor National Park headquarters.

Bridge Street - The date 1845 appears in the cobbles outside the Bridge Inn (3) while near the old smithy opposite

is a notice recording the height reached by the waters of the Lynmouth floods of 1952-3. Forge Cottage dates from the 17th century while off to the left, along Town Leat, stands the 3-storey Town Mills building (4), once a busy corn mill.

Fore Street - On the left are the library and Exmoor National Park information office and a footpath leads to the Guildhall Heritage & Arts Centre (5) which offers historical displays, exhibitions and the Exmoor Photographic Archive. On the right of Fore Street, which used to host the town's fairs and markets, are the arched steps of the 1866 market hall (6), altered to its present form in 1930.

Lady Street - At the end left are a chapel and mill (7), the latter a fulling

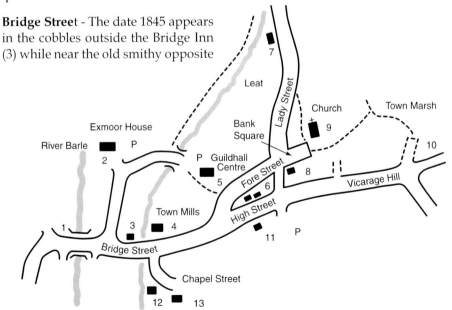

mill turned paper mill and also associated with Dulverton's early electricity supply. The street also has a pump and bollard dating from the mid 19th century but not on the original site.

Bank Square - Attractive buildings include the period No. 3 left and the Lion Hotel right (8), the latter with the Natwest Bank beyond.

The Church - Offering an excellent vantage point as it stands benignly overlooking the town this attractive building (9) dates mainly from a reconstruction of 1852-5 although the tower dates back to the 15th century or earlier. Note the 1907 lych gate.

Town Marsh - There was a smithy here and an old handpump and waterwheel survive (10) at the Vicarage Hill end.

High Street - Is a mixture of cottages plus one or two larger buildings, including the attractive Barle Gallery (11). Sydenham House, on the opposite side, dates from the 16th century or earlier and was formerly a farmhouse. At one time its was owned by Sir Francis Drake.

Chapel Street - The leat runs alongside the street to serve Dulverton Laundry (12) and then the Lower Mill beyond. The former manufactured blankets until about 1830 and then converted to crepe production. Later it stood idle for some ten years before becoming a laundry in 1871; the latter was a grist mill. Further on is the Independent (Congregational) chapel, hall and schoolroom (13) dating from 1831.

At an ancient crossing point of the River Barle this bridge forms part of the reason for Dulverton's very existence.

23

DUNSTER

HISTORY

Dunster is a place of history and contrast, a bustling town in the summer when visitors crowd the High Street shops or attend events at the castle, and a quiet village out of season when normality returns. Overlooked by the castle and by the wooded slopes of Grabbist Hill and Vinegar Hill, the town offers much of interest, from the oft-photographed yarn market to the quieter tithe barn and the working water mill. Although it is some distance away on the other side of the busy A39, Dunster has its own beach and even a station on the preserved line of the West Somerset Railway.

There have been Iron Age and Roman finds around Dunster but it was left to the Normans to see the potential of the valley of the River Avill for developing a small agricultural settlement with access to the sea and secure beneath the walls of the castle built by the Mohuns soon after the Conquest. Dunster's harbour was first mentioned in 1183 and by 1222 the town had its own market which increased in importance as cloth manufacture grew apace and fulling mills occupied several sites along the river.

Medieval Dunster occupied the area around Church Street and High Street. In parallel with the commercial activity of the town, its early church grew in importance with the arrival of Benedictine monks from Bath in the 12th century to establish a new church building and priory and then to influence local life until Dissolution in 1539. By then trade was being lost to Minehead and Watchet due to the silting up of Dunster's more modest harbour but the "broadcloth called Dunsters" remained popular enough to warrant the building of the Yarn Market in 1609.

The 17th century was not a good time for Dunster. The Luttrells, who had bought the castle for 5,000 marks in 1376 and funded much change and rebuilding, chose the wrong side in the Civil War. Barely had the town started to recover from a bout of plague in 1645 than it was inundated with Parliamentary troops intent on the lengthy siege of the castle which eventually led to demolition of all but its residential part. After the Monmouth Rebellion two Dunster men were hanged on Gallows Hill.

Happily Dunster did recover from its tribulations and many of the

In front of Dunster's Church of St George stands a venerable building embodying medieval features and the remains of the former priory.

24

present buildings have 17th century origins. More building followed in the 18th and 19th centuries as Dunster grew with the agricultural exploitation of Exmoor and then its discovery by Victorian visitors intent on exploration and leisure. Taken together all these various influences have shaped a township which offers history and interest wherever you look.

THE WALK

From the car park and Visitor Centre in The Steep head up The Ball and turn left down Priory Green. At the corner take the footpath on the left across the churchyard to West Street. Walk along West Street and turn left along Park Street to the packhorse bridge. Take the footpath to Mill Lane and the water mill before returning to West Street. There, retrace your steps and turn right into Church Street, left into High Street and then right back to the car park.

GAZETTEER

The Ball - Has a number of pleasant cottages including Nos. 1 and 2 (1) which are 18th century. The Priory Gate House stands a little further on.

Priory Green - Leads to a 16th century tithe barn (2) on the left and a well preserved dovecote (3) opposite, its 8.5m height and 4.5m diameter typical of 13th/14th century examples but probably contemporary with the barn. Priory Lodge and Old Well Cottage are on the corner and remnants of the former Benedictine Priory are embodied in Nos. 5 and 7 which stretch back into the churchyard.

St George's Street - Has a mixture of thatched and other cottages of which Nos. 15, 17 and 19 (4) are 17th century with later alterations. The Primary School (5) dates from 1871 but The Rectory is a modern building. The stump of a butter cross stands at the Minehead end of the road on the site of a 14th century preaching cross.

The Church - The present church of St George (6) is mainly 15th century with some earlier works and a major restoration in 1875. Its great rood screen once separated the monks' portion and originated from one of

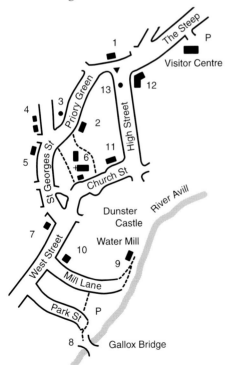

the many differences between them and the townsfolk. There are the remains of a 15th century cross in the churchyard.

West Street - Woollen workers used to live in this street and in 1645 wall openings were made in some of the houses to permit movement without exposure to plague in the streets. On the east side Nos. 1, 17, 27 and 29 date from the 17th century as does No. 24 opposite, the rest being variously of the 1700s and 1800s. No. 2 is a former 1878 Methodist Chapel (7).

Park Street - The 15th century Gallox packhorse bridge (8) is at the end and gallows once stood nearby. Several cottages, including Nos. 24 to 30, are 17th century.

Mill Lane - The corn mill (9), now restored to working order, is on a medieval site but dates from the 17th century with extensive rebuilding in 1779-82. At the West Street end stand the 1825 Wesleyan Day School (10) and a former poor house.

Church Street - Nos. 26 and 28 left are again 17th century but Nos. 4-8 (11), the so-called Nunnery, are two hundred years older. This splendid row of three jettied and timbered storeys belonged to the Abbots of Cleeve and was probably used by priory guests. In between, No. 18 is a late medieval priest's house, much restored c1877.

High Street - The varied and interesting buildings of this street, once the market area, are mostly 18th and 19th century with Nos. 6 and 19-23 from the 17th. The Luttrell Arms (12) right was an inn by 1651 but is much earlier while the Yarn Market (13) opposite, octagonal with central and outer stone pillars supporting a slate roof, was set up in 1609, repaired 1647 and restored more recently.

The oldest castle building is the 13th century gatehouse, most of the main buildings dating from 1600 onwards, with remodelling in 1869-72. The Castle Hill buildings are mostly 17th century, with jettied No. 6 a 19th century rebuild. At the other end of town the Conygar Tower is a c1775 folly. It looks down over the exhibition, information point and shops of the Visitor Centre area.

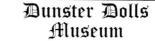

GLASTONBURY

HISTORY

Within today's bustling township there is still plenty to affirm Glastonbury as a place of mystery and legend. Having grown out of the Vale of Avalon, on a raised site around the great abbey and below the dramatic Tor Hill it is not hard to believe that Joseph of Arimathea might have buried here the Cup of the Holy Grail and planted his staff in the soil of Wearyall Hill to create a tradition of midwinter thorn blossom. Equally credible is the idea of Arthur and Guinevere and their last great native kingdom of the post-Roman era.

Whatever the truth Glastonbury was undoubtedly one of the last outposts of the old gods and an early outpost of the new.

The earliest certain church dates from around the 7th century with St Dunstan then developing an abbey around it that was to continue, through the Norman period, until the complex was destroyed in a great fire of 1184. Henry II started the rebuilding process shortly afterwards and the abbey continued to grow in size and influence until Dissolution in 1539 and the dreadful day when Abbot Whiting was hanged on Tor Hill and his body quartered for display in other Somerset towns.

The influence of the abbey stimulated agricultural and commercial activity in central Somerset and placed Glastonbury on the main traffic arteries of succeeding centuries. Flemish immigrants were quartered in the old abbey grounds and first woollens and then silks became important. The Civil War brought both rebels and royalists to the town, several of the former being hanged in the High Street after their defeat. Later years produced a brief period as a spa town and then the arrival of the Glastonbury Canal around 1833 and of the Somerset Central Railway over the same route twenty years later. Drainage of the surrounding moors affected the commerce of Glastonbury with tanneries appearing in 1868 and 1870 to begin a major trade in hide and skin products which still survives in specialist form along with today's multiple light industries.

Glastonbury is centred round Magdalene Street, the Market Place and High Street.

On one side are the remains of the great abbey and on the other St John's Church, built in the 15th century on the site of an earlier Norman building. High Street typifies the mixture that is Glastonbury with impressive period buildings like those of the George & Pilgrims Hotel and The Tribunal rubbing shoulders with more functional stone bank buildings, a host of brick houses-cum-shops, some nice town houses and the odd delights of an ornate Victorian shop front or the drama of the United Reform Church.

Well worth a visit are the Tor, topped by the 14th century St Michael's Tower, Chalice Well Gardens, the Somerset Rural Life Museum, the Lake Village Museum and the remains of the abbey complex.

THE WALK

Explore the Market Place area, head up High Street and then turn right at each major junction to complete the square made up of High Street, Lambrook and Chilkwell Street, Bere Lane, Fishers Hill and Magdalene Street. Short additional excursions up Bove Town, further along Chilkwell Street and down Benedict and Northload Streets will all prove rewarding.

In the centre of Glastonbury is this 19th century replacement for the medieval market cross and adjacent water conduit.

GAZETTEER

Market Place - Early 19th century Northload Street joins the Market Place with two late medieval timber-framed buildings, Nos. 1 and 2 (1). The latter is slightly jettied and has intriguing corbels. Nearby the ornate market cross (2) dates from 1846. Down Benedict Street Nos. 4 and 4a are probably late medieval and the church dates from a rebuilding around 1520.

High Street - Adjoining the late 18th century banks on the left stands the fine panelled frontage of the George & Pilgrims Hotel (3) which originated in the 14th century to cater for abbey guests and pilgrims who stayed

Typical of the variety in Glastonbury's High Street is this contrast between the solid, plain bank building and the elaborate style of the George & Pilgrims Hotel, once an abbey hospice.

beyond their free hospitality period. The Tribunal (4) beyond, now housing the Lake Village Museum, was begun well before its 1500 Tudor facade and was a court or a merchant's house. In the Perpendicular style, St John's Church (5) is 15th century and has a fine tower. Its churchyard is now the home of the Glastonbury Thorn.

On the right the wonderful Victorian shopfront of No. 10 (6) is next to the arch of the old White Horse Inn where defeated Monmouth rebels were hanged in 1685. A passage leads to the 1864 Assembly Rooms. Further up the street No. 48, Nos. 51-63 and 88-90 are probably 17th century and also worth noting are No. 31 the c1700 Town Clerk's Office (7), the mock half-timbered No. 30, the 1938 Post Office and the splendidly

uncompromising porch of the United Reform Church of 1814/1898 (8).

Lambrook Street/Chilkwell Street - Left of the Summer House nice cottages lead up Bove Town, past the Gospel Hall. A cottage on the north side was once the medieval pilgrimage chapel of St James. Right of the Summer House stands an old fountain urging "Commit No Nuisance" and the Methodist Church (9). Avalon Hall, ex chapel and then Parish Rooms, stands on the corner of Silver Street with a simple but fine No. 17, The Vicarage, opposite and the exuberant Abbey House (10) beyond.

Chilkwell Street has late medieval (Nos. 43 and 45), 16th century (51 and 53), 17th century (2, 4, 16-22, 30 etc) and a variety of other buildings ranging from the ornate Chalice Leas (11) to two nice Victorian villas. Where it skirts Chalice Hill, gardens contain the chalybeate waters of the spring (12)

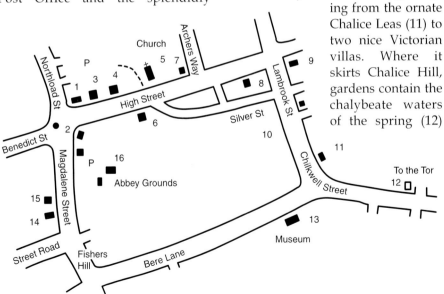

which once fed the abbey complex and the spa and are now a place for rest and reflection.

Bere Lane - The front building of the Rural Life Museum is the fine 14th century home barn of Glastonbury Abbey (13). Beyond are period and modern cottages.

Fishers Hill / Magdalene Street - On the left before Street Road is the modest 1897 Victoria Nursing Home building and after it a mixed but interesting 17th century group (Nos. 40 to 50). Then follows St Margaret's Chapel and Almshouses (14), the chapel originally part of a 13th century medieval hospital with tiny almshouses added inside the hospital walls at a later period. Next comes a cottage group which became the Pump Room (15) in 1752 to serve Glastonbury's modest spa period. Either side of the Roman Catholic church are some substantial stone houses - Copper Beech (once a hotel), Abbey School and Somerset House.

On the right just before the car park and abbey entrance is a massive ornamented casting presented by J. Henry Burgess to commemorate his 6th mayoralty. Then comes the rather plain 1818 Town Hall. The abbey remains (16), consisting mainly of St Mary's Chapel, the Abbot's Kitchen and the Abbey Church, warrant a separate visit.

 visitor information

If you would like to know more about travel to the area, places to stay and attractions to visit please contact one of our *Tourist Information Centres*

South Somerset, Petter's Way, Yeovil Tel: (01935) 471279 Fax: (01935) 434065
Podimore, A303 Services Tel: (01935) 841302 Fax: (01935) 841294
Chard, Tourist Information Centre Tel: (01460) 67463

or *Local Information Centres* at

Bruton, Dovecote Building	**Castle Cary,** Market House	**Crewkerne**, Town Hall
Tel/Fax: (01749) 812851	Tel: (01963) 351628	Tel: (01460) 57294
Ilminster, Local Information Centre	**Langport**, Langport Library	**Somerton**, Market Place
Tel: (01460) 73441	Tel: (01458) 253527	Tel: (01458) 274070
Wincanton, Wincanton Library		
Tel: (01963) 34063	*or visit our website:* **www.southsomerset.gov.uk**	

ILCHESTER

HISTORY

The northern approach to Ilchester via the Fosse Way is through its twin settlement of Northover, over the River Yeo and into the market square where the two main streets of the town divide. Except when an aircraft from Yeovilton roars overhead the town is a quiet, unpretentious sort of place and it needs a little imagination to picture it as first a sizeable Roman settlement and later the county town of Somerset. Roger Bacon was born here in 1214 and Ilchester was the early home of the 18th century poet Elizabeth Rowe.

There was an Iron Age settlement just south of present-day Ilchester and finds of pottery by the River Yeo suggest occupation long before the Durotriges tribe was overwhelmed by Vespasian's Roman troops in the first century AD. The military probably built an early fort to guard the river crossing and meeting point of the Fosse Way and the Bristol-Dorchester road. Rome then brought prosperity to Lindinis via these roads and a river harbour with a later fort east of the river and with buildings throughout the present town site and all along its approach roads. Ilchester was undoubtedly a large and important civic centre in the Roman and Romano-British periods and two sizeable cemeteries have been identified.

There was a gradual decline when the Romans left but revival began in the late Saxon period when Ilchester appears to have been an adjunct of the royal estate at Somerton. The town was steadily rebuilt with stone from the old Roman buildings and by the time of Domesday had over 100 burgesses. It had a mint from 973AD and by 1086 the market was the largest in Somerset. Charters in 1183-4 and 1204 led to further expansion and the town gained a hospital around 1226 and a Dominican Friary a little later. A new wall with gates along the four main approach roads was built from Roman wall rubble about this time and enclosed an important community with at least six medieval churches. Ilchester became the prime town of Somerset until this distinction passed to Somerton for ninety years around 1280.

By the time its county town status returned Ilchester was smaller than Northover and its Jewish trading community had fled. However, a new gaol was built in 1371, the courts returned and new mills began to operate. There was a further charter in 1556 and a new gaol in 1599 but apart from brewing and a few other minor industries the town was dependent mainly on its administrative eminence and local agriculture. The failure of a canal scheme, agricultural changes and the loss of the courts and gaol activity in the 1840s were body blows and, with no railway to stimulate alternatives, Ilchester became a quiet backwater.

Today's Ilchester, freed from the frenzy of pre-bypass traffic, has a lot of history and some pleasant and interesting buildings. Some of its housing originated as a result of vote-rigging in the years before the Reform Bill and some from the temporary affluence which accompanied the replacement of the old corporation with town trustees in 1886-9. Along with the town monuments, the houses of the prosperous and the very real sense of past prominence, the mix is an interesting one.

THE WALK

From Ilchester Bridge pass right of the market cross and down High Street. Continue along West Street to Pill Bridge Lane and then return to turn right into Almshouse Lane. Return to the bridge by turning left into Church Street and continue ahead to Northover church and back.

GAZETTEER

Ilchester Bridge - A 7-arch medieval bridge built here around 1200 was largely rebuilt in 1797 and widened in 1932 (1). It once had gaol and chapel buildings and the town's North Gate stood nearby.

Market Place - Castle Farm (2) on the right stands on the site of an 1813 inn behind which once lay the medieval Whitehall Nunnery. Beyond that is the former waterside trading area. Ahead are the Town Hall and Community Centre (3) in a building dating mainly from 1812-16, the Bull Inn which replaced the 1669 Sun Inn and corner buildings which were at one time banks. The market cross (4) was erected in 1795 in place of an earlier cross. The 18th century Ivelchester Hotel/Ilchester Arms (5)

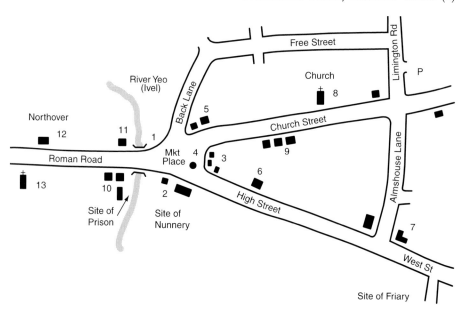

left is a solid, attractive building with a fine Tuscan porch.

High Street - The Ilchester Museum on the corner, and once the post office, is well worth a visit. A little further on the left is the 18th century Dolphin Inn (6) and opposite are pleasant terraced cottages of c1820 in English garden wall bond.

West Street - On the left stands the so-called Manor House block (7), including its attendant service wing, with more cottages on the right. The area behind these once housed a Dominican friary the ruins of which were later used as a silk mill. Pill Bridge Lane, once the medieval route to Long Sutton and Langport, takes its name from a 17th century, 3-arch packhorse bridge and was privately turnpiked for a period.

Almshouse Lane - The 1426 almshouse foundation once stood on the left corner, near the old West Gate. Further along were three of the town's eight inns.

Church Street - On the corner Bos House was formerly the Cow Inn. Beyond it on the right stands the Early English style St Mary Major church (8) with its squat octagonal tower containing some Roman bricks. The chancel dates from the 13th century but the building was considerably enlarged in the 15th. Behind Warwick House next door a cheese factory once stood on the Bartons site. There is an 1867 cottage at the end and then modern housing on the

former manor house site. On the other side of Church Street (9) stands a former 1850 Methodist chapel (9).

Roman Road - Behind the substantial period houses on the left (10) once stood the huge prison complex of which only two cottages now survive. From 1811 hangings took place in the prison gateway beside the river. Opposite, Mill House (11) marks the site of a mill which operated from the 12th century to around 1816. Further on right is the Northover Manor Hotel (12) which started life in the 17th century as two cottages. The church of St Andrew (13) on a mound opposite is 14th or 15th century but the site was used for worship long before and has probably been in use since Saxon times.

This hamstone market cross in the centre of Ilchester was erected in 1795.

33

ILMINSTER

HISTORY

Ilminster lies in a sheltered area between the River Isle and the twin Pretwood and Herne hills in South Somerset. Its minster church occupies a commanding position in the town whose name means "the minster on the Isle". This *mother* church, which was strongly linked with the abbey at Muchelney, originated in Saxon times with the early town growing up in the area around the church and along today's Silver Street to the market place. By the time the Normans came it already had three mills and a thriving market which Domesday records as paying 20 shillings a year. In 1201 the direction of religious supervision and tribute then changed from Muchelney to Wells but Ilminster's commercial growth continued with the addition of a 2-day annual fair to the weekly market.

Despite a serious fire in 1491 Ilminster prospered in the late medieval years. Today's splendid church was built, a grammar school established and new houses added to the original cluster. By 1670 the town was the fourth largest in Somerset with woollen broadcloth becoming increasingly important in the next two centuries and commerce booming in parallel with the rise in coach traffic along the nearby London-Exeter road. One of Ilminster's visitors was the Duke of Monmouth who was joined by 57 local recruits in June 1865, but 12 of the rebels later paid for their enthusiasm on the gallows.

The making of ropes and gloves added to Ilminster activity in the 18th century with some of the profits being ploughed back into fine houses. The Chard Canal reached the town in 1841 and the Great Western's branch railway from Taunton in 1866, both bringing cheaper coal to provide power for new industries, which included those based on hemp, flax, tow, silk and bricks. Pottery, an early Ilminster speciality, was joined by collar-making around 1862.

Today Ilminster remains an active and attractive town. At its heart is the open market place with banks and business gathered around it. Nearby the splendid minster is the centre of a group of period buildings of high architectural interest and in the warm, honey-coloured hamstone of the area. The town has a variety of modern light industries, ranging from stone products to specialised instruments, but also retains some delightful period shop fronts.

THE WALK

Leave the Shudrick Lane car park in a northerly direction for the Market Square and then turn left into Silver Street. Circumnavigate the church before continuing ahead along West Street and eventually returning along High Street. Another right into North Street leads back to the market place where East Street can be explored before returning to the car park.

GAZETTEER

Ditton Street - On the west side is the single-storey, 7-bay former collar works (1) and on the east the old Swan Hotel (2) where the Court of Royal Peculiar was held until 1857.

Market Square - The market house (3) with its Tuscan colonnades dates from an 1813 rebuilding. There is an old drinking fountain and stone water conduit nearby.

Silver Street - The buildings are mostly 18th and 19th century and include delightful shop fronts on each side. Greenfylde School (4) left has a Gothic frontage and was built in 1878 (enlarged 1894) to take over from the original Ilminster Grammar School. A pump and old inn buildings stand on the right just beyond the church.

The Church - The minster church of St Marys (5) is like a small cathedral with a fine central tower and much elaboration - pinnacles, gargoyles, canopies, buttresses and the like. It stands in the centre of a green churchyard and community of older buildings.

Court Barton / Church Walk - The Chantry (6) on the left was a medieval priest's house, rebuilt around 1840 and with neighbouring cottages dating back to the 17th century.

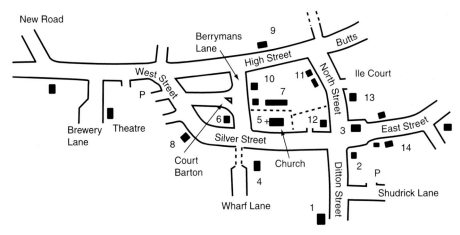

35

Ilminster's main roads meet at the Market Square where this early 19th century market house is an outstanding feature.

Behind the church is a delightful group (7) of further chantry property including the medieval Cross House, the Old Library, the School and the Vicarage. The school building was "occupied by Ilminster Boys' Grammar School 1549-1878 and the Girls' Grammar School 1879-1971", the headmaster using Cross House after the Reformation. Note the various inscriptions, dates and sundial.

West Street - The 18th/19th century houses have attractive frontages. Note No. 24, the lowered causeway and the very distinctive Ashley House (8). Before returning go as far as the attractive 1887 Methodist Church and take a look down Brewery Lane.

High Street / Strawberry Bank - The Bell Inn (9) is 17th century, as are Nos. 14, 29 and 31. There is a raised causeway left and the ugly Gospel Hall right.

Berrymans Lane - Down here are the Masonic Lodge (10) and Abbot's Court dating from the 18th century but with earlier origins. They were once part of the old Court Hall and Abbot's Court was used as a Writing School at one stage.

North Street - On the right is St Mary's Hall followed by a row of thatched cottages (11). Parts of Nos. 9 to 13 are 17th century. The former George/Victoria Hotel (12), now flats, goes back to pre-1664 and retains its sign recording the young Queen Victoria's first hotel stay on December 23rd 1819. Notable on the east side of the road is the Victorian Gothic stone frontage (13) inscribed "National Daily and Sunday Schools, erected by voluntary subscriptions AD1853".

East Street - On the south side are Boots mock half-timbered building and the massive 3-storey NatWest bank (14). Opposite are collar factory buildings and those of the magistrates' court. In the angle with Frog Lane is the Old Meeting House (15) of the Unitarian church, now used for exhibitions and other local events. The nonconformist activity here dates from 1672 and the building from 1719. Further up East Street Nos. 42 and 52-60 are 17th century houses.

Ilminster has its own small theatre in the former brewery building in Brewery Lane. Also worth seeing are the remaining traces of the Chard Canal at the end of Canal Way.

The Roman bricks incorporated in the tower of St Mary Major church at Ilchester are a reminder that it was once an important Roman settlement

One of several attractive period shop fronts in Ilminster.

LANGPORT

HISTORY

Modern Langport still reflects the town's past role as the centre of mid-Somerset commercial activity. The River Parrett made Langport a distribution point for the whole area from the 15th century onwards, this role being vastly accelerated in later years, especially after the setting up of the Parrett Navigation Company in 1836 and the subsequent deepening of the river to allow larger vessels to reach the town. Two names stand out in Langport's 18th and 19th century prosperity, those of merchant Samuel George Stuckey and maltster Thomas Bagehot. Together they developed Langport's distribution role, set up the Langport Bank (later Stuckeys) and at one period were involved in operating over 30 local barges and East India vessels.

Further back in time Langport's strategic location below the junction of the Parrett and the Yeo brought several periods of conflict. As a Saxon *burh* and fort protecting the Somerton royal estate it was sufficiently impor-tant to have its own mint but almost certainly saw fighting with the Danes. Then Langport forces unsuccessfully resisted the Normans and got involved in the struggle between the rival forces of Stephen and Matilda. Later the town was fined heavily for lending support to Perkin Warbeck's Cornish rebels. Worse was to come in the Civil War when, after three days of manoeuvring and skirmishing between the opposing forces, the Royalists set fire to Bow Street as they retreated towards the river and safety.

Langport is recorded as having a market in 1344 and there were several religious houses there. At one period the town had four annual fairs and the Corporation established by Elizabeth I's charter of 1596 lasted until 1883 when Town Trustees took over. By then most of the buildings owned by the Corporation and the Lord of the Manor had been sold to life lessees and the proceeds used to improve roads, gardens and open spaces. The town got a new Bow Bridge in 1840-41 and a railway in 1853. The old divisions between Huish Episcopi and Langport and between the church and market on the hill and the other market in Cheapside became less important as modern Langport emerged, full of charm and historic interest.

The routes down The Hill -probably the site of the Saxon burh - and North Street lead to the commercial centre of Langport and then along the Bow Street causeway to the river and the old yard, wharf and warehouse areas around Bow Bridge. The whole route is lined with buildings which testify to the busy and varied past of Langport and contribute to its present air of activity and prosperity. At the bridge end, on the old station site, the Langport & River Parrett Visitor Centre holds much of interest.

The old Register Office at Langport stands at the top of Bow Street, an ancient causeway which leads down to the River Parrett.

THE WALK

Three routes radiating from the shopping centre car park provide access to the town's high interest - along Cheapside and up The Hill to the hanging chapel and back, then a short trip along North Street and finally down Bow Street to Bow Bridge and back.

THE GAZETTEER

The Hill - On the left of the ascent is the c1800 rectory in red brick Flemish Bond, the Roman Catholic complex of St Gilda's Court and Christian Centre (1) and East Gate Cottage, a reminder that a gate in the town wall once stood below the Hanging Chapel (2). The latter originated in the 13th century but has later alterations and it has been, in its time, a chantry chapel, the town hall, the grammar school, an arms store, Sunday School and Masonic Lodge. Next come the 1827

Old School House with barge boards and mullioned windows and its companion the Old Police House. Returning on the south side is the Church of All Saints (3)which originated in the 12th century and was rebuilt in the 15th. Walter Bagehot, founder of The Economist magazine, has a tomb in the churchyard. There are 19th century cottages nearby and The Gateway (4) whose first deeds are dated 1672. The Old Grammar School at the end of St Gilda's Close also has an interesting gateway.

North Street - Some houses survive from the 1834 fire and date back to the previous century making the street an interesting mixture embracing tiny cottages, the c1840 Stone House and the Black Swan Inn (5) of 1727 or earlier.

Cheapside - On the north side stand the 1732-3 Town Hall (6) in red brick with Ham stone ashlar dressings and owing its existence to a loan from the Portreeve, the Royal British Legion

Cheapside at Langport with the 16th century Langport Arms on the right.

39

Club which started its life in 1833 as a reading room, and the 19th century Register Office. Opposite are the original premises of Stuckey's Bank, now the National Westminster, the 16th century Langport Arms Hotel (7), later refronted, and the 1826 birthplace of Walter Bagehot. The other buildings in Cheapside also repay scrutiny.

Bow Street - This was originally an ancient causeway from Cheapside down to the Parrett and its houses have a tendency to be less well supported at the rear! Over the years countless tons of coal, lime, salt, fish, timber and other goods must have been hauled along here from the wharves at Bow Bridge and the character of the street, which is where the river bargees used to live, still reflects this past activity.

Along the north side of Bow Street the pump of one of several artesian wells (8) survives, a tribute to the 1878 workmanship of LeGrand & Sutcliffe of London. Then, at the end is the entrance to the former quay and

warehouse and what was probably the wharfmaster's house (9). Next comes Great Bow Bridge (10), built in 1840-41 for £4,200 in local lias stone ashlar with three arches and on a bridge site dating back to 1220.

Further industrial buildings survive on the south side of the bridge along with the town and river visitor centre. The 18th century Old Custom House (11) Inn was previously The Angel and the court leet was held here to decide matters like grazing on the town's three common moors. Further on, The Dolphin Inn was first mentioned in 1778 but has a later frontage. Most of the other houses and shops along this side are late 18th or early 19th century.

Other locations of interest in and around Langport include a foundry building and ironmaster's house in Beard's Yard, the entrance and buildings of the former Kelway's royal nurseries in Somerton Road and, at Huish Episcopi, the 12th century church and Pound Cottage, Hurd's Hill which has 15th century origins.

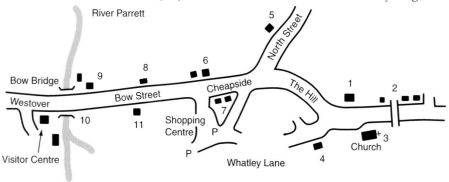

MARTOCK

HISTORY

The long streets of Martock display much of interest and character, with a significant number of venerable buildings in the warm hamstone of the area that seems to come alive at the least touch of sunlight. It is true that roistering Parliamentary troops did some damage to the church when celebrating the fall of Bridgwater in 1645 but, this apart, Martock's history has been mostly calm and tranquil.

Today's town lies on what was the edge of the vast Saxon forest lands. It had no great significance at that time but just grew slowly through the centuries, drawing benefit from the adjacent Fosse Way and River Parrett but not being overwhelmed by the traffic of either. Domesday records a manor and fisheries here, but of no large size or national importance, and the original Martock settlement seems just to have emerged out of the needs of a largely agricultural community.

This early village must have attracted more attention and status when it became the home of the Treasurer of Wells Cathedral and this would be further enhanced with the addition of a new central hall to his home around the year 1290. Before long the community needed a school and by the early 1500s life was prosperous enough to permit replacement of the old church by a fine new one. In 1661 the earlier school of 1636 was succeeded by a free grammar school in the court house and the passing years added further to the town's prosperity and to its collection of fine houses - it is especially rich in 17th century farmhouses. Two posting inns served the stagecoach era and the Martock & South Petherton United Turnpike brought improvements to four of the local roads.

The 19th century saw considerable growth and change in the area. Enclosure took place early in the Hundred of Martock and by the 1830s the town was also a major glove manufacturing centre. Bad harvest years forced the emigration of some of the local paupers but then sawmills, sailcloth works and agricultural engineering joined the glovemaking activity to increase the number and variety of local jobs and bring money into the town economy. The expansion was helped by the arrival of a broad gauge railway in 1849 although its opening was then delayed for four years.

Today's Martock continues full of activity but this cannot detract from a basic serenity that derives from a long and wholesome history of which so much evidence is apparent in the enviable collection of very fine buildings of every kind.

THE WALK

From the car park off North Street first explore right and then return towards the Market House and turn left to explore East Street. Return and turn left to explore the east side of

Church Street and Water Street. Return on the other side, past the church and then along a footpath left to Ashfield Park and back to the starting point.

GAZETTEER

North Street - The oldest house is No. 84 which may be as early as the 15th century.

The street starts with two substantial blocks and a modern library on the right (1) and individual older houses left. Then come smaller stone dwellings and Nos. 45 and 47 which were the Old White Horse Inn (2), the Old Farriers, the Old Police House and the Old Bakehouse. The latter dates from the 17th century as do Nos. 2, 12, 85 and 87. The Methodist Church (3) left was built in 1886.

Market House & Pinnacle - The market house (4) dates from the 1750s

Modelled on the famous Pillar of Trajan, Martock's 1742 Pinnacle stands beside its Market House contemporary.

and used to consist of butchers' shambles below and assembly rooms above. It was restored for council use in 1960-1. The Pinnacle (5) of 1742 occupies the site of a medieval cross.

East Street - Beyond the small green and its cottages on one side and the White Hart Hotel and post office on the other, East Street is dominated by former 17th century farmhouses on the right - Welmans and Byron House (6), The Yews (7), Nos. 25 to 29 (8) and then Madey Mill farmhouse and mill (9). The latter is a 17th century watermill with medieval origins.

Church Street - The old Manor Farm outbuildings (10) down the lane on the right found new uses for glove manufacture and as the 1930 home of the fire engine. Since the first hand pump of 1755 this had formerly been based in the Market House.

The Manor House (11) itself dates from 1679 but was largely reconstructed after a fire in 1879. It is followed by the Parish Hall, the 1893 Gospel Hall and the home of chantry priest (12) funded by John de Soy in 1325. The pleasant George Inn (13) is 19th century but parts date back at least to 1631. Next is "Martock National School House" of 1846 and then the venerable Treasurer's House (14), now owned by the National Trust. Much altered over the years, the house was first mentioned in 1226. On the west side note Church Lodge (15) and Nos. 14 to 18 of the 17th century.

The Church - The 15/16th century parish church of All Saints (16) with its notable 1513 roof and interior features is on a Saxon site but was much restored from 1860.

Water Street - On the south side Pattenden on the corner is part of the former vicarage site. The Doctor's Old House (17) is similar to but slightly younger than the late 18th century

(19) has a long and complex history and bears the legend 'Neglect Not Thy Opportunities'. It housed Martock's first two schools and has also served as court house, poor house, church house and library in its time

Pound Lane - On one corner stand the old stocks and a church gateway recording its 1627 churchwarden benefactors. On the other is Ashlar House with the 17th century Clerk's House beyond.

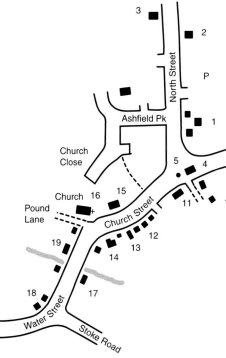

Ashfield Park - Behind the modern houses note the substantial former home of Martock landowner William Cole Wood built some time prior to 1849.

While in the area visit the craft centre at Yandle's Works on the B3165 to the south of Martock. West along the South Petherton road are the Parrett Works which retain industrial buildings associated with the former flour, flax and ironworks activity there.

Bridge House on the next corner. Opposite both the Old Butchers and the Old Bakery (18) have vehicle entrances and are followed, nearer the Pinnacle, by The Grange group. The worn stone of the Court House

PORLOCK

HISTORY

Beyond Minehead the A39 road heads east through the fertile Vale of Porlock to the small town from which it takes its name and the following 1 in 4 climb up the notorious Porlock Hill on the way to the Somerset border with Devon. The poet Southey records that Porlock was known as the "End of the World" because of the barrier represented by this climb where the motor vehicle was unable to replace horse transport until well into the 1920s. Today all that has changed and Porlock is easily accessible to the many who visit this pleasant Exmoor township and its seaside extension at Porlock Weir.

Although the busy A39 road runs through the heart of Porlock it has not spoiled the attractive appearance of the town.

The modest Porlock Weir harbour, one and a half miles west of Porlock proper, helped to make the area important in Saxon times. It was raided unsuccessfully by the Danes in AD918 and again by vengeful Saxons after the Norman Conquest but then settled down to the routine of catching fish and handling small trading vessels. Around the Porlock area sheep farming on the hills gave the town importance as a wool centre in the Middle Ages with a market area in the High Street, adjoining shambles and a cottage industry based on spinning yarn for the Dunster manufacturers.

After a period of high prosperity in the 16th and 17th centuries the wool trade declined, although the weekly market and annual fairs, first granted in 1366, lasted until the 19th century. In the fields around Porlock barley, wheat and oats continued as important crops, along with cider apples, but the town became more concerned with charcoal, tanning and the use of the finished leather. By 1840 a directory was emphasising the importance of the "importation of coal and lime from Wales". At this period Porlock's population stood at 838 and the community had four shops and four inns as well as maltsters, saddlers, tailors and the shoemakers who used the leather from the town's tannery which in turn was fed with the bark of local oak trees. In the 1920s the population first rose above 1,000 and began to include those offering "board residence" to the increasing number of visitors to Exmoor.

Today agriculture remains important in Porlock with the National Trust even re-introducing some of the old cider apple types like Tom Putt and Sheeps Nose. Alongside this role Porlock now welcomes and provides for thousands of visitors each year and the shops along the main road reflect their needs and interests, adding colour and activity to the older buildings and cottages which portray the town's history and origins.

THE WALK

From the car park at the eastern end of High Street explore Doverhay and then walk the length of The Drang. Explore the church and Parsons Street before walking the remainder of High Street as far as the Visitor Centre. Return on the opposite side to the starting point.

GAZETTEER

Doverhay - On the corner is the Dovery Manor Museum, well worth a visit and housed in what was probably the manor's dower house (1). Some original features of the 500-year

old building were preserved by a restoration of 1894-5. Further up the lane Doverhay House (2) carries a 1690 date.

The Drang - On the right stands The Gables, another building in the ornate cottage style so often portrayed on calendars. Further on, at the church end, is Chantry Cottage (3) which housed the succession of Cleeve Abbey monks whose task was to pray for the Harrington family in the church chantry. Note the period wooden doorway.

The Church - Despite the truncation of its spire this is an attractive 13th century church (4) with Saxon origins and embracing a fragment of original Saxon cross. It is dedicated to the Welsh St Dubricius who, according to Geoffrey of Monmouth, officiated at the wedding and coronation of King Arthur. In the front churchyard stand a 15th century cross and the remains of an ancient yew tree, said to be 1,000 years old.

Parsons Street - Rising to the hills behind Porlock, this street offers a

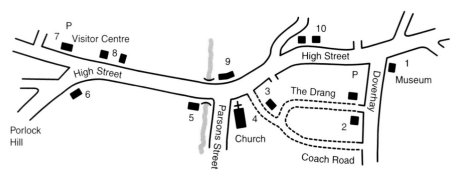

46

A variety of sailing boats nestle in the approach to the small harbour at Porlock Weir.

pleasant walk towards Hawkcombe via the rectory, the old school and the former rector's mill.

High Street - On the left heading west is the former manor mill (5), now part of an art shop. This area, by the Castle Hotel, was once the scene of Porlock's regular markets and fairs. Further along, in the part of High Street which precedes Redway and Porlock Hill, is the Ship Inn (6) where Southey stayed and which used to be the starting point for the coaches climbing the hill. Just along the road to Porlock Weir an old school houses the combined visitor centre, parish room and information point (7).

Returning along High Street note Myrtle Cottage (8) which carries a 1604 date and two fire insurance plates. Nearby are the 1927 Methodist Church and the entrance to the old tanyard. Further along, opposite the church, stands the old Rose & Crown building (9), a former inn noted for accommodating R.D. Blackmore and for closure due to rowdiness in 1880. On the section back to the car park there are two more 17th century inns, the Three Horse Shoes and the Royal Oak (10), the former now replaced by the Lorna Doone Hotel.

While in the area take a trip to Porlock Weir. Heavy gates protect a small harbour within the shingle beach behind which there are cottages, accommodation and a few smaller shops selling some remarkably fine products, including locally blown glass. There are also a blacksmith's shop and a hatter's premises.

SHEPTON MALLET

HISTORY

Known particularly for its drinks industry, fashion and retail furnishing, Shepton Mallet is an attractive, well-balanced town combining much of historic interest with modern residential, commercial and light industrial functions. The town offers great variety, from the imposing Anglo Trading Estate building to the gaunt walls of H. M. Prison and from weavers' cottages to the old mills along the River Sheppey. Many old mill buildings remain, some with their attendant manor house and workers' housing.

Early settlements surround Shepton Mallet. There have been Bronze Age finds at Cannard's Grave but its clearer history begins with the arrival of the Romans via the Fosse Way where there was probably a service town. In Saxon times *Sceapton* was the subject of a charter under which King Ina granted lands in the valley of the River Sheppey to the Abbot of Glastonbury in AD705. This ecclesiastical involvement continued under the Normans with the Malet nobles then giving the village its suffix. Eventually Shepton Mallet was made part of the Duchy of Cornwall in 1536.

Mendip sheep brought a growing prosperity to Shepton Mallet in the Middle Ages, cloth and woollens being sold at the fairs and markets established by charters of 1235 and 1318. Skilled workers arrived from Europe after the Black Death and as many as 30 mills prospered along the course of the Sheppey from Charlton to Darshill. The original medieval area around High Street and Town Street was then expanded east along the river valley following the building of the House of Correction in 1625-7.

By 1642 Shepton was involved in Civil War skirmishing and it later became the base for the Roundhead commander Sir Thomas Fairfax. On June 23rd 1685 the town welcomed the Duke of Monmouth but twelve of its citizens were later to hang in the Market Square as the price of this support.

When the wool trade moved north Shepton Mallet, along with many other Somerset towns, suffered quite badly. Combined with the effects of the Napoleonic wars much poverty and unemployment resulted, even rioting. However recovery eventually came, mills converted to silk, velvet and crepe, breweries were set up and the town began to produce a wider variety of goods. Improvements in transport followed the setting up of the Shepton Mallet Turnpike Trust in 1753, the arrival of the East Somerset Railway in 1858 and of the Somerset & Dorset in 1874.

The 19th century revival was typified by the building of the Anglo-Bavarian Brewery in 1864 to produce one of Europe's first lager beers. The clothing mill at Charlton became a brewery and Showerings converted from shoe making to brewing in Kilver

Street. Opposite, the crepe mill became Jardine's model lace factory from 1907 until 1922. Quarrying, rope, bricks, tiles, shoes and bacon curing products were all important at various periods. In more recent years the conversion of the Anglo-Bavarian to a trading estate typifies the changes in Shepton Mallet where the market place area has been revitalised and industry and commerce thrive, often in older buildings

THE WALK

From the Old Market Road car park head for the town centre via Commercial Road and turn left into High Street. Take a look along Great Ostry left before exploring the market place area and exiting along Town Street. At the end cross Rectory Road to Tipcote Hill and explore both Draycott Road and Cowl Street before heading east along Longbridge and Lower Lane to Leg Square. Leave this via Peter Street, pass around the west side of the church and then turn left into Gaol Lane and right into Frithfield Lane. Cross Paul Street and take the path through Collet Park to Park Road. Two right turns and one left then lead back to the car park.

GAZETTEER

Commercial Road - Attractive buildings are the combined court house and police station (1) of 1858 and the 1801 Independent, now Baptist, chapel (2). The *Anglo* building (3) dominates the section beyond the crossroads.

High Street - Most of the buildings in this varied street date from the first half of the 19th century, although Nos. 47, 61 and 68 were built around 1750. At one time there was a mountebank

This is the imposing building of the former Anglo Bavarian Brewery which revived the Shepton Mallet economy when it opened in 1864.

49

and preaching stage outside the Bell Inn, itself of c1850.

Great Ostry - On the right is an interesting terrace of 3-storey clothiers houses (4) dating from c1650, the half house at the end being the result of road widening.

Market Place - A fountain built of four different stones stands in front of the Market Cross (5) and Shambles, the latter with covered market tables of a type used from the earliest times. Parts of once-arcaded shops survive and Nos. 10 and 11 are timber-framed houses of c1600. The Market Cross was

built c1500 in memory of Walter and Agnes Buckland, the open arches being added later.

Town Street - The earliest buildings are Nos. 7 and 9 which date from 1798, the others being very slightly later. At the end right is the ornate, balconied "Liberal Club and Mechanics Hall" (6). Town Street and its Waterloo Road extension, developed after the building of the bridge in 1826, were formerly the main road to Bristol and Bath.

Tipcote Hill - Once a place of picking, spinning, weaving and dyeing with three mills, Georgian houses and an inn to serve the thirsty.

Draycott Road - Industrial buildings on the left are followed by the Masonic Hall and the tall, evocative Sales House (7). This mid-Georgian complex, formerly a woollen mill, mansion house, shops and cottages, was later used by a convent of visitation nuns.

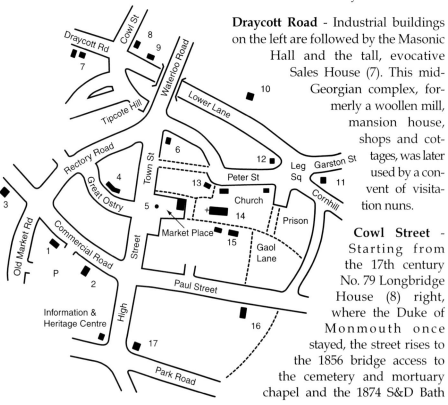

Cowl Street - Starting from the 17th century No. 79 Longbridge House (8) right, where the Duke of Monmouth once stayed, the street rises to the 1856 bridge access to the cemetery and mortuary chapel and the 1874 S&D Bath

Extension railway viaduct. The houses range from period craftsmens' cottages right to small modern houses left with the 1696 Unitarian Chapel set back higher up.

Longbridge - On the left Nos. 2-5 (9) are attractive Jacobean 3-storey houses of around 1675. Opposite is No. 12 of 1750 and former industrial buildings.

Lower Lane - Still shows evidence of the activity powered by the tiny river which a footbridge crosses to cobbled Barrendown Lane. The narrow section contains a surviving part of Sherrings Brewery also used when the dancing bear came to town and then the Georgian Barren Down House (10) of c1800 and set back on the left.

Leg Square - In the angle between Garston Street and Cornhill is Town Mill (11) which in its time has produced woollens, silk, corn and bakery products. Just up Garston Street on the left is the Kings Arms complex, once the haunt of quarrymen and supplier of beverages to the prison up Cornhill. The prison has a near continuous history since 1627 but in World War II was used as a military *glasshouse* and for the safe storage of documents like the Domesday and Magna Carta papers. Opposite Town Mill is Eden Grove (12) c1750, with a further mixture of houses, cottages, the Old Manor House and a spite wall in the southern arm of the square.

Peter Street - Beyond No. 20 The Hollies and the assembly rooms of c1800 is the rear of the Old Grammar School complex (13) with, on the left, No. 27 The Old Manse, The Rectory and the end school building inscribed "Disce aut discede" (apparently "Learn or leave"). The route to the church reveals the remainder of the Old Grammar School group which originally was founded by the clothier Strodes in 1627 who provided a schoolroom, master's house, chapel and accommodation for four widows.

The Church - Commenced on a Saxon site in the 14th century the church (14) has a notable 350-panel *waggon* ceiling. The capped tower was intended to have a spire.

On the south side are more charity buildings (15), the 1862 Bread Room for distributing bread and the 1699 Strode almshouses next door.

Paul Street - No. 1, No. 9 and Nos. 14 to 20 date from around 1750, the Wesleyan chapel (16) was built in Doulting stone in 1810 with No. 28, its manse, slightly earlier and No. 4 Park School c1870. Note also the former warders' cottages.

Park Road - Has a former milling complex behind Highfield House with The Tall House (17), where John Wesley used to preach, on the corner with High Street.

Also of high interest are the mill buildings in the Kilver Street area and at Charlton where the 17th century clothing mill became a brewery and is now a business park. An 1800 toll house of the Shepton Mallet Turnpike Trust survives on the main road.

The 3-storey houses in Longbridge at Shepton Mallet date from c1675 and the prosperous years of the town's woollen industry.

At the heart of Somerton, opposite the church, stand the 17th century Town Hall and its companion Market Cross.

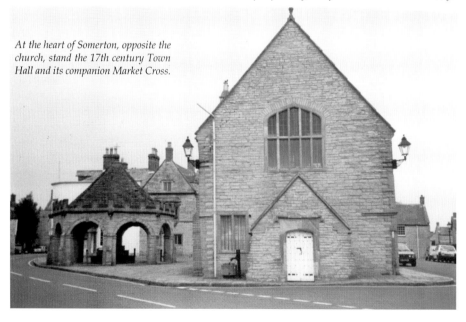

SOMERTON

HISTORY

This quiet, dignified town reveals something of interest wherever you look. Its attractive buildings of local lias stone have a rare richness and variety which imparts a sense of the town's long and honourable history and make its exploration a delight.

The Romans passed by Somerton on their way to Street, leaving the small settlement to rise to prominence in the Saxon era. It was the home of the Somersaetas tribe and Ina, great king of the West Saxons, made it a royal town. The Danes then undid all this, burning Somerton after Alfred's defeat in 877AD but the town was rebuilt and by 949 was hosting the Witan, the great assembly of the Saxon king's advisors.

Somerton enjoyed a continuing importance after the Norman Conquest, first becoming a borough and then gaining a market in 1255. By 1278 it was the chief town of the area, site of the shire courts and gaining a county gaol two years later. Much of it was rebuilt about this time but the county town status reverted to Ilchester in 1366 leaving Somerton to develop its role as a market centre for the surrounding agricultural community, something it has continued right up to the present day.

The 17th century brought Somerton a market hall and market cross to facilitate the trade at its Tuesday markets and periodic fairs. Animals were sold in The Square, Kirkham Street, Broad Street, Cow Square and North Street, with buyers then sealing their bargains in one of the town's plentiful hostelries. Some of Somerton's earliest inns and houses date from the 17th and 18th centuries with the 19th then producing schools and churches, a brewery, banks, gasworks and a fire brigade. The 1900s began with a smallpox outbreak in 1905 but the railway arrived in 1906, the wireless station in 1926 and the milk factory in 1927.

Today some of these older activities have gone but Somerton has added a tourist role to its retail business, light industry and traditional agriculture.

THE WALK

From the Square or the Brunel Shopping Precinct walk along the south side of West Street to the Triangle and return along the precinct side. Explore the Square and the church before turning left into Broad Street to reach Cow Square. Continue ahead along North Street to the roundabout and then return to New Street. Turn right at the end and return via The Millands and Kirkham Street.

GAZETTEER

West Street - The modern Brunel Shopping Precinct (1) uses buildings of the old brewery and stands opposite the 1803 Congregational (now United Reform) church with its "Lecture Hall" entrance and school-

53

rooms to the right. Further along the south side of the street are the 1626 Sir Edward Hext almshouses (2) where blind windows and doors mark an 1883 conversion from eight dwellings to four and an inscription proclaims "He hath dispersed abroad and given to the poor; his benevolence remaineth for ever". The Hext Court extension at the rear was added in 1983.

On the north side return note the Old Bakery and the Unicorn Hotel (3) which has been an inn since at least 1756 but existed well before that. Note also the c1500 Leavers Court, the former school buildings and the 1845 Wesleyan Chapel.

The Triangle - Around this area are an old brewery, a mill house, Zion Chapel (4) and Salvation Army School Room together with the site of the former milk factory, bombed in 1942 with the loss of nine lives.

The Square / Market Place - Much rebuilt, the Market Cross dates from 1673 when it replaced a 14th

century predecessor. Its companion Market/Town Hall (5) started life about 1688 as a single storey market house, altered in 1719 and serving variously as a meat market and magistrates court with lock-up. Across the road is the memorial hall (6) and a plaque recording the town's role in the Monmouth rebellion when seven rebels were hanged here. On the left are Sir John Strangeway's 17th century house and Lloyds Bank (7) which stands on the site of the Great House.

On the south side of the square the 18th century White Hart (8) has medieval origins and the Globe starred in The Monocled Mutineer. Selwood House was once a preparatory school. The east side is dominated by the former Red Lion Hotel (9), once a coaching inn with central entrance to former stables and servants' dormers above. Other

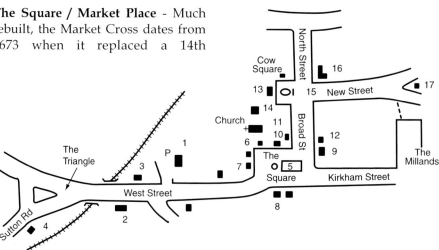

54

notable buildings in the square include the 16/17th century Market House (10), Freeman House and Old Bell House.

The Church - St Michaels and All Angels (11) north transept arch is 13th century, the nave 14th and the magnificent timber roof - possibly carved at Muchelney Abbey - 15th or early 16th. A major restoration took place in 1889.

Broad Street - Store cattle and pigs were formerly sold here at the Rother Beast Market hence the extra road width and central gutter. Collars were produced in a factory next to Collar Cottage and opposite the 1676 Free Grammar School (12) and the 1708 house now used as a bank. Also on the east side is a varied terrace including The Narrow House, Craigmore House (c1700) and Medwyn House.

Cow Square - The Old Town Hall (13) has a double Mansard roof and may well be the site of the original Hall of Pleas and county gaol. Behind lies the Vicarage (14), a stately building with medieval origins but much altered in 1815. In front of the Old Town Hall stands a fine oval yew hedge with some venerable 1770 buildings on its north side and, ahead, the decorative Coalbrookdale horse trough-cum-drinking fountain-cum-gas lantern (15) celebrating the delayed coronation of Edward VII.

North Street - Starting with Mrs Sophie Scott Gould's almshouses (16)

of 1866, this short street offers a fine collection of 17th and 18th century cottages including Jacob's Well/The Old Armoury and then Turle House named after a noted Somerton-born organist and composer.

New Street - New in 1349, this was later the route of the Langport, Somerton & Castle Cary Turnpike. Several dwellings have ecclesiastical connections but not Cockspurs (17), once Somerton's oldest inn and housing a cockpit in the roof. Note the attractive Old School House.

Kirkham Street - In the days when cattle were sold in Broad Street and Cow Square, pigs in North Street and sheep outside the church gate, Kirkham Street specialised in horse trading.

Along this old route out of Somerton, new in 1349, stands Cockspurs, once an inn and cock-fighting site.

SOUTH PETHERTON

HISTORY

All along the Fosse Way, today's A303 trunk road, there are small towns and substantial villages located just off the highway, far enough away to avoid the heavy traffic but near enough to enjoy the access benefits such arteries bring. South Petherton is just one such township, lying just north of the main road and just west of the infant River Parrett in an area of South Somerset blessed with rich soil and thriving agriculture. At one time the route from Petherton Bridge, where the main road crosses the river, west through South Petherton and on to Shepton Beauchamp was a turnpike highway but this was later declassified, allowing South Petherton to regain its sturdy independence and traditional lifestyle.

Roman villa remains have been discovered near South Petherton and there is coinage evidence pointing to the existence of a mint in the pre-Norman years of Edward the Confessor. Domesday does record a manor at Petherton but the early history of the settlement, which owed allegiance to the priory at Bruton for many years, does seem to have been concerned primarily with serving its large agricultural community. Ten years after Civil War troops had damaged the church, South Petherton was recorded as a market town with 300 families but in later years neither canal nor railway saw much profit in its business. The result was the independent growth of an active, self-respecting township, full of self-reliance and creating a pleasant legacy for today's visitor.

A jewel in the South Petherton buildings' crown is the fine church with its unusual octagon tower while King Ina's Palace, a 19th century manor house on a much earlier site along the road to East Lambrook, fittingly maintains a link with the years of Saxon royalty. A number of buildings bear witness to the agricultural tradition - Shutler's Mill on a Domesday site in North Street, Joyler's grist mill and Shaw's flax mill at Petherton Bridge; and a 17th century farmhouse survives in Palmer Street. Other buildings record a past social structure - the Court House, the Under Sheriff's Office and various houses built for the gentry.

Attractive and interesting 15th and 16th century buildings in St. James Street at South Petherton.

On the semi-industrial front South Petherton used to have twine and brick works and the town has a long history of glove-making which employed 434 women and children in 1851. In 1859 it had 20 shops and a daily wagon to Bridport for the sack and canvas trade. Today the main activities are retail and the provision of the sort of general services demanded by an active rural community.

THE WALK

Park in Prigg Lane, turn left along Knapp Hill and right into South Street. Another right into Hele Lane will lead to the church and Market Place. Explore West Street and Crown Lane. Exit via the cobbled footpath near the former Crown Inn, turn right at the end of George Lane into Palmer Street and right again to return to the car park along the length of St James Street.

GAZETTEER

Knapp Hill - The pleasant former ecclesiastical group on the lower corner (1) includes the 1863 main church building, now used for community purposes, the manse and the church hall.

South Street - Knapp House (2) at the junction of Knapp Hill and South Street was originally two houses. It is followed by a pleasant and venerable group on the left (3) including No. 3 of c1672 and inscribed "Samuel MacMillan Licensed Tea Dealer",

No. 5 of 1741 with its delicate portico and the long Nos. 7 and 9 which originated in the 17th century but were later remodelled. Older houses beyond include No. 27 of c1700.

Hele Lane - A pleasant byway crossed by the waters of the adjacent chalybeate spring.

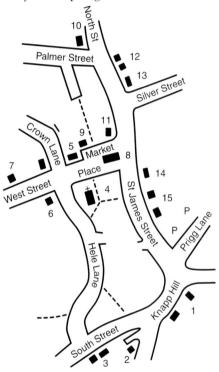

The Church - The Anglican parish church (4) , perched benignly above the market place, is full of interest. The site has Saxon origins but the present building dates from the 13th and 15th centuries, although its record of incumbents goes back to 1080. Pioneer Methodist Thomas Coke,

In a dominating position in South Petherton's Market Place stands the Blake Hall, opened as the Liberal Club in 1912 and a memorial to William Blake JP.

who had a house in St James St, was once a curate here but left in 1771 amid angry scenes.

West Street - Starting with the former under-sheriff's building (5) opposite the war memorial, this is a street of pleasant, venerable houses and cottages. No. 1 on the left (6), The Old House, was once set amid large grounds and was the home of a solicitor. Note also Denmans, Monk's Corner and The Vineyard (7), formerly two cottages and a cider house. Just down Crown Lane on the right is a fives wall.

Market Place - Dominating its surroundings is Blake Hall (8) former "Liberal Club" and built in 1911 in memory of William Blake. It replaced

the 1843 market house and lock-up. The old Crown Inn (9), thatched and a fire victim at one time, has been converted to residential purposes but retains its coach entrance.

Palmer Street - Both No. 10 and the Palmer Street Farmhouse, or Shutlers, date from the 17th century. Opposite, the Old Meeting House once stood in the grounds of Rock House. The Methodist Church (10) on the corner maintains a nonconformist tradition that came to South Petherton in 1753, built its first chapel here in 1809 and the present building in 1881.

St James Street - On the west side of this main thoroughfare the houses are mainly 18th and 19th century and include a modest building labelled

The Market House (11) and the meeting room built by public subscription in 1828 as a boys' charity school.

On the other side, starting from Palmer Street and progressing southwards, there is first the U-shaped Nos. 48 and 50 Court House complex (12) where the older wing started life as a functioning court house in 1540 or earlier. Even earlier than that is the Nos. 40 to 44 group (13) which was once a parsonage but has undergone much change and rebuilding over its 500-year lifespan. After the bank and The Old Bakehouse is the Brewer's Arms (14) which began life around 1622 but was rebuilt in 1925 after a major roof fire. Among the gentry houses are No. 14 Norris House (15), once the home of Hugh Norris, medical man and noted local historian, and then No. 6, the 1771-77 home of Thomas Coke, first bishop of the American methodist church.

Now a night club, this 1920s cinema was one of Street's first brick buildings.

Old pump

STREET

HISTORY

Street is located at the eastern end of the Polden Hills, where this narrow upland meets the low, flat moorland of the Somerset Levels. Overshadowed by its neighbour Glastonbury in earlier, ecclesiastical years, today's town of Street has a distinctly different character derived in large part from the influence of the Clark family and the shoe-making activity which, over the years, has gained an enviable world reputation.

The town's High Street is full of commercial activity and colour, with every kind and quality of footwear on offer, but the pleasant grey-blue lias stone used in so many of Street's buildings ameliorates the minor excesses of modern marketing and gives the whole town a welcoming and planned look. The relatively recent Clark's Village complex of shops has brought in more visitors and added to Street's popularity and prosperity.

In pre-history ichothysauri roamed the area around Street and thoughtfully left their bones for the benefit of the local museum. Much later the Romans provided one of their precision roads on an alignment similar to today's Glaston Road and left evidence of settlement around the church. Subsequently both the Saxon and Norman eras also left traces. Records of the 12th century point to a sizeable sheep population around the town and it seems likely that Street was following the pattern of other Somerset towns in converting wool and skins to meet area clothing needs. A windmill existed around 1250 but, less pastoral 400 years later was the death of 25 Royalists in a Civil War skirmish just along the Somerton road.

Just before restoration work on the old church began in 1826 fell-monger and wool-stapler Cyrus Clark began to experiment with making rugs. He was soon joined by his brother James who introduced the idea of using discarded smaller skins for making slippers, soon popular and known as *Brown Peters*. From such modest beginnings sprang a whole new industry which financed a Friends' Meeting House in 1850 and in later years gave Street a whole range of fine buildings, from the Board School of 1859 to the Institute and Crispin Hall in 1895.

The Clark business grew rapidly by using American machinery and establishing a system of commercial travellers to sell the output which, by 1860, was more than 200,000 pairs of shoes a year. Tanning and other specialised processes were carried out in factory premises but all finishing was done by out-workers with the packed products then being carted to Glastonbury station for despatch. The population of Street grew rapidly, from 500 to 2,000 and then to 3,500 with Clarks providing several streets of advanced housing that remains attractive to this day.

This century has brought further change including concentration of work in the factory buildings and the use of computer technology. Other businesses have also thrived in the Street atmosphere and the town also accommodates several parts of Millfield School and the Strode college, swimming pool and theatre complex, all making a contribution to a lively and attractive town.

THE WALK

From any of the car parks behind High Street walk along the left hand side of this thoroughfare in a north east direction. Turn left at The Cross and right along the length of Brutasche Terrace. Turn left into Glaston Road, right along The Mead and right again into Church Road. Return to the starting point via High Street with a short deviation down Wilfrid Road and back via Leigh Road.

GAZETTEER

High Street - The United Reform Church (1) and its linked manse and mixed barge boards offers a pleasant start to the left hand side of the street. The main buildings date from 1866 and the rear extensions from 1884. The "Street Vestry Room 1860" stands across the road while on the opposite corner is the old Board School (2), built as a British School in 1859 using profits Clarks made from the Crimean War but which their principles led them to plough back into the community.

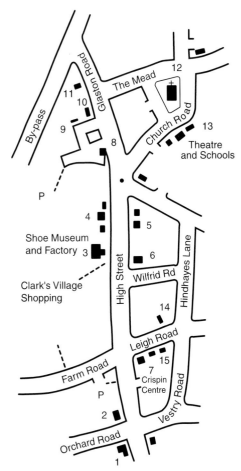

At the far end of High Street the factory group(3), including the shoe museum, is made up of Clark's House of 1855, the clock tower of 1887 and the main frontage and water tower of 1897-8 and then the 1933 extension with its large *more light* windows.

Further on are Nos. 48 and 48A, once a 17th century farmhouse, the 1850 Friends' Meeting House (4) and No. 26, the 1810 Goss House.

On the opposite side of the road Nos. 17 and 19 originated as 17th century cottages while the Mullions Hotel (5) goes back a further century and was once the centre of Street. The 1894 Bear Hotel (6), another nice building and another Clark enterprise, started life as a temperance hotel. Much further along, on the corner of Leigh Road, is Crispin Hall (7) built with Clark money as a social and cultural centre.

Grange Road - The junction with The Cross is now occupied by the remains of a lamp and drinking fountain (8)

Rising above the Bear Hotel are the clock and water towers of Clark's factory.

made by the Sun Foundry, Glasgow and presented by Miss M.A. Ansell in 1893. The area is one of model housing groups e.g. The Chestnuts 1893, The Acacias 1892 and The Hollies 1903 but at the end of Brutasche Terrace is a rare surviving tollgate (9) purchased from the Wells Turnpike Trust in 1883.

Glaston Road - On the left are the 1814 Baptist Chapel (10) and a former tollhouse (11).

Church Road - This is the former Roman area, now leading to the Church of the Holy Trinity (12), the anglican parish church which dates back to the 14th and 15th century and has some surviving medieval glass. It was restored in 1826 and again in 1843. Nearby are Bowlingreen Mill and the college, school, theatre and community complex (13).

Wilfrid Road - Nos. 1 to 23 make up a terrace of workers' housing dating from 1885. Lawson Terrace was built in 1891 and Cobden Terrace in 1889.

Leigh Road - On the left is the 1924 Library and then the former 1920 Maxime Cinema (14), in a brick and stone design very typical of its period. On the right are the 1893 Methodist Church (15), the 1887 Vestry Rooms and then Crispin Hall.

Behind the Clark's factory complex lie the shopping delights of Clark's Village.

WATCHET

HISTORY

At the most southerly point of the curve of Bridgwater Bay stands the ancient town and port of Watchet. Modest in size, it occupies a shelf of level ground between three small hills and the mud and sand foreshore that fronts the Bristol Channel. On the west side of the town the Washford River finds its way to the sea while inland rise the wooded slopes of the Brendon and Quantock Hills.

The history of Watchet goes back in legend to the distant years of the 5th century when the Celtic Christian missionary St Decuman crossed from Wales in a coracle and built himself a shelter near the town. His preaching was less than well received and Decuman was beheaded by the local

The varied buildings in Watchet's Swain Street include, centre left, the former iron and brass foundry.

inhabitants. Unfazed by this setback he recovered his head, washed it in the waters of a well near the present church and replaced it on his shoulders, producing instant wonder, remorse and conversion among his hearers.

Less reliant on legend is the evidence of a small town and fort at Watchet in the 9th century. It clearly suffered a series of Scandinavian raids, especially in the last years of the 10th century, but survived sufficiently unscathed to establish in the reign of Aethelred II (AD976-1016) a mint that was to go on producing coins well into the Norman era. Around this period the original Saxon burh on Cleeve Hill headland was affected by erosion leading to the establishment of a new settlement on the present site. By the 13th century this had become a borough and obtained a market charter although the port at Watchet seems to have been languishing.

In the Tudor years Watchet prospered in its market town role, its silted harbour was cleared out and its ships sailed regularly to and from Ireland, but the number of vessels using the harbour then declined again as Minehead grew in importance and took over the Watchet cattle trade. Despite this, fishing remained important along with the export of kelp and the import of Welsh coal. From 1750 papermaking joined the age-old agricultural and cloth production activities of the area.

Everything changed with the formation of the Brendon Hill Iron Ore Company in 1853 to exploit the deposits up on the Brendons west of Raleghs Cross. A railway link down to Watchet was developed over the years 1856-61 with two new harbour piers added in 1862 for shipping the ore to South Wales. The main line railway arrived at the same time and the town prospered, with a variety of small industries including shipbuilding.

In this century Watchet has had its share of changes with the port losing first its iron ore and, more recently, the flows of timber, car parts, paper and tractors. Today papermaking has been joined by light industry and there is a new focus on a marina development and on the tourist activity which is supported by a good service of tourist trains on the reopened West Somerset Railway.

THE WALK

From the Harbour Road car park exit to Swain Street and turn right. At the end turn left into Market Street and left again after the river. Leave the footpath by turning left into Mill Street and Anchor Street and then cross to Harbour Road and follow its course beside the railway to The Esplanade. Turn left there and left again into Swain Street to regain the car park.

GAZETTEER

Swain Street - The street is mainly 19th century, the West Somerset Hotel (1) - home to early theatrical events - being built quite early in those years but having later alterations. Also on the left are the Post Office, No. 28 which is the 1730s Bank House (2) and then a former iron and brass foundry building (3).

Market Street - In this area, which once housed the cross, the shambles and the pillory, the surviving Market House (4) replaced an earlier such building in 1820 and was provided with a small Court Leet lock-up under the stairs. It now houses the town's excellent museum which includes a model of the mineral railway and its 1 in 4 incline up to Raleghs Cross. A hauling post for the old lifeboat stands outside. Elsewhere in the street, No. 1 is at least 200 years old while The Bell was first mentioned in 1744. Shantyman Yankee Jack lived at No. 18.

Mill Lane / Street - Mill Lane runs parallel with the Washford River starting with the Old Station House (5) and remains of the mineral railway platform on the right. Nearby are the Star Inn and the Old Mill (6). A small stone footbridge in Mill Street crosses the river and leads via 17th century cottages to the variety of Anchor Street. The period buildings of the former Mill Farm and Stoates flour mill (7) stand east of the river while the route of the old mineral railway is marked by the direction of Whitehall.

The Cross - The council offices (8) stand on the left at the top of Swain Street and consist of a modest house with *Elizabeth II* clock and an RAF Regiment war memorial in the form of an extension to the building. There are other interesting houses and atmospheric alleys nearby.

Station / Harbour Road - The preserved West Somerset Railway and its traditional station (9) and stone goods shed (now a boat museum) are on the right and on the left the handsome 1871 Methodist Church (10). Above Brendon Road are the Salvation Army building and the 1824 Baptist church.

The Esplanade - On the corner a plaque records the legend of Watchet's founder St Decuman. The library building (11) is on the site of a shipbuilding yard dating from the period of iron ore mining. It was erected in 1875 to house Watchet's first rowing/sailing lifeboat, the Joseph Soames. Next is the 1930s style Ritz cinema building (12), then a former farmhouse area and, at the end, some half-timbered cottages (13), one with a barometer set into the wall, the "Gift of Sir A.A. Hood".

On the seaward side are the landing slip and the eastern and western piers protecting the harbour where the Watchet Hobblers used to pilot the iron and coal vessels in and out and where a stranded Royalist vessel was once seized by a troop of Parliamentary horsemen. To the right is a row of 1800s coastguard cottages and a lookout tower.

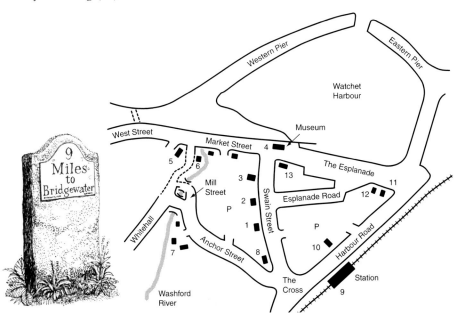

Visit Watchet

Somerset's Ancient Harbour Town

✪ Market House Museum

✪ Boat Museum

✪ Steam Railway

✪ Plenty of shops and places to eat and drink

✪ A unique old world port

✪ Cliff walks and Old Mineral Line

✪ Tropiquaria - tropical house and aquarium

✪ Good choice of places to stay

For more information contact:
West Somerset Tourism (Watchet)
Council Offices, Williton, Taunton TA4 4QA
Tel: 01984 635208
Fax: 01984 635257
E-mail: wsdced@netcomuk.co.uk

Or visit Watchet Tourist Office on The Esplanade, Watchet at Easter or between May and September

WEDMORE

HISTORY

Wedmore is a small town of great charm and with a venerable place in its country's history. This it owes to King Alfred who spent the early years of his reign struggling to keep the Danish invaders out of Wessex and then seized the initiative after a remarkable victory in Wiltshire in 877AD. From the resultant position of strength Alfred was able to come to an agreement with Danish Guthrum in a ceremony of baptism and pledge in 878AD which culminated on the heights of Wedmore and became known as the "Peace of Wedmore". Before this the area had been known to the Romans and it was later to feature in Domesday but never again was it to achieve such status or to play such a part in the stabilisation of our emerging nation.

Edward the Confessor granted Wedmore to the Bishop of Wells elect and this ecclesiastical connection was to dominate community life for centuries. Wedmore had a church from the 11th century and it was the summer residence of the Deans of Wells throughout the medieval period. There were major landowners like the Hodges and the Horlers but Wedmore developed primarily as a yeoman agricultural community with a weekly market and two annual fairs. By the 16th century it was providing schooling and care for the sick and destitute. Hannah More opened a school in the town in 1799 but was not very flattering about its inhabitants.

Wedmore agriculture has generally thrived throughout the years, land enclosure being extensive and early. But the town's position on an island of high land meant increasing isolation as contemporary towns began to

The view from Wedmore's church yard reveals buildings from three centuries with the Mendip Hills in the background.

67

Contrasting styles in Wedmore; the chemist's shop displays a strong Italianate influence while the small villa has a wealth of decorative features including some oyster-shaped tiles.

prosper from the freer movement of goods along turnpike roads and then the arrival of cheaper coal along the moors waterways. In some desperation Wedmore set up its own turnpike trust to improve links to Bristol and Taunton, unfortunately rather late in the turnpike era.

The enterprise that had given Wedmore its first market charter in 1255 and sustained its slow but steady growth over many centuries has resurfaced in recent years and the town now draws visitors from a wide area to its specialist retail outlets. The Borough Mall, a small but pleasing dedicated shopping development, stands in pleasant and varied surroundings, its callers staying to enjoy the fine church, market cross and wide range of Wedmore buildings, from modest stone cottages to large Italianate villas.

THE WALK

First explore Church Street and Cheddar Road. Then return to the junction and head along The Borough with right turns following into Grants Lane and Glanville Road. Now take left turns to traverse Pilcorn Street, Guildhall Lane and Sand Road and then return to the starting point.

GAZETTEER

Church Street - The parish church (1), laid out in the shape of a cross, is largely 15th century although its beautiful south doorway area is much earlier. There was a major restoration in 1880. An attractive war memorial (2) stands at the main entrance to the churchyard, with a 15th century preaching cross (3) on the opposite side. Most of the churchyard yew trees have markers commemorating royal and other notable events of the last 150 years. Also recorded is the unearthing in March 1853 of a crock containing some 200 coins "of the time of Kings Ethelred, Canute and Harold", the notice adding "there is nothing covered that shall not be revealed". Next to the church is the George Hotel (4) with its coach entrance and mounting block. The present 18th century building, in stone and to a very pleasing design, replaced a much older inn. The north side of the street ends with a fine group (5) comprising the former assembly rooms, built in 1866 by public subscription, the Italianate 1830s chemist's building, once a fashion house but now without its tearoom tower, and a pleasant and colourful cottage-villa with decorative dormers and barge boards.

On the other side of the road the Old Vicarage (6) has 15th century origins and may be on a Saxon site. Note the Post Office shop frontage and its varied companions.

Cheddar Road - On the left is the church schoolroom (7) with the country house style vicarage beyond. Holdenhurst (8) on the opposite side of the road is a mid-18th century property with stable, coach house, summerhouse and grotto.

The Borough - Among the 17th to 19th century buildings along the road, several show further Italian influence and contrast with the part-jettied Swan Hotel and the modern shopping mall. Beyond the latter stand Cross Farm and then a worn but fine market cross (9), dating from the 1300s and once the centrepoint of the Tuesday market and the July and September fairs. Then come the 1845 Lerburne House and the 16th century Barnards cottage group at the end.

Grant's Lane - Another notable house, of 1841, stands opposite the elevated 1857 Baptist Chapel (10) left with its attendant schoolroom and graveyard. A varied and attractive

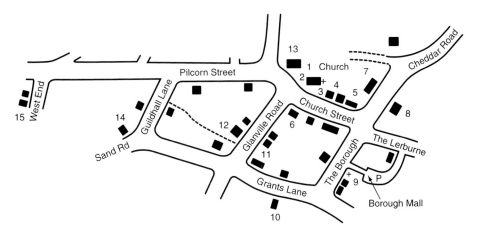

group of dwellings (11) stands on the right at the end of the road.

Glanville Road - The road takes its name from the builders of the towered Elmsett Hall (12) left. This is followed by Glanville House with Beggar's Roost and Buoy's Cottage, 16th century and once a school, right and the tiny Lerburne stream below.

Pilcorn Street - The "Manor" group (13) by the church is a fascinating mixture with a history going back to 1334. Further along on the right stands a grape press gift from St Medard marking the 20th anniversary of twinning. Older houses on the south side include Rustic Porch which dates back to the late 16th

century and Fernside, believed to have been a Hannah More school.

Guildhall Lane - Midway on the right is a former slaughterhouse while Sunset Well opposite had a reputation as a holy well. At the end Hall Farm stands on the left with the 1817 Wesleyan Methodist Chapel (14) round the corner on the right. Ornate windows and a double-door portico relieve an otherwise severe building.

The walk can easily be extended to West End where a delightful group of 17th century stone buildings includes Gogs House, Porch House (15), The Close and Westovers, built by John Westover in 1680 to house and care for the mentally ill.

This tiny Toll Cottage survives at Williton as a reminder of the days of the turnpike trusts.

WILLITON

HISTORY

Like neighbouring Watchet, Williton suffered at the hands of the Danish invaders in the second half of the 10th century, the known site of one battle being the aptly-named Battlegore where ancient bones have been unearthed in a field beside the road to Watchet. The town also shares St Decuman, the early Celtic missionary, with Watchet, the Williton church of St Peter originally being a chapel attached to the larger establishment of its neighbour. The two did not always see eye to eye.

In the Norman years Williton was part of a substantial but sparsely populated manor held by the FitzUrse family, but then half of it was given to the Templar Knights of the Order of St John of Jerusalem as a gesture of atonement for Sir Reginald's part in the murder of Thomas a Becket in Canterbury Cathedral. In 1363 the remainder passed to the Fulfords and eventually to the Wyndhams, ancestors of the last Earl of Egremont. They purchased and developed the Orchard Wyndham estate just to the west of Williton. A very old house survives there in private hands along with a farmhouse and other buildings from the 17th century.

The town itself also has several 17th century farmhouses to testify to its agricultural heritage and there were both grist and fulling mills in the area.

An annual fair for toys and hardware began in 1767 and lasted until 1877. Williton was undoubtedly saved from being a rural backwater by its position on the main east-west turn-pike route of the Minehead United Trust and the junction there with the turnpike route to Taunton. Schooling in the town is recorded as far back as 1645 and by 1835 the number of schools in Williton had grown to eight day schools and four Sunday schools.

Then came the formation of the Williton Poor Law Union in 1836 and the building of a workhouse shortly afterwards, bringing in its wake both status and employment for the town. The Union covered 36 parishes and employed a master, matron, chaplain, medical officers, school staff and relieving officers. Further expansion followed with the West Somerset Free Press giving the area its own news-paper from 1860 and the arrival of the main line railway from Taunton two years later. The railway still survives as an active preservation scheme carrying regular trains of tourists in the summer.

Always busy with traffic on the A39, Williton is a long, straggling town but one full of interest and ful-filling important functions both to its own community and to the summer visitors who call there or make it their holiday centre.

THE WALK

Park in Killick Way, turn left on leav-ing and then right into Bank Street.

Explore the church area after turning left into Bridge Street and then follow the street until it joins the main road. Turn left along High Street, right along Fore Street and right into Long Street. Then continue on the left as far as the former workhouse and return on the opposite side to regain the car park.

GAZETTEER

Bank Street - The stumps of two crosses (1) stand at the roundabout junction next to the substantial NatWest Bank building (2) in red sandstone. Opposite is the Egremont Hotel (3), built in the 1820s on the site of an old coaching inn. Prior to the building of a separate court in 1858 justice was dispensed here to the prisoners confined in a nearby lock-up.

Priest Street - Just beyond the Egremont Hotel are Nos. 4 and 5 (4), the former an ornate, towered police station once occupied by a superintendent, a sergeant and two constables, and the latter a court-house which later housed the public library. Both are by John Morton and date from 1858. Nos. 12 and 14 nearby are 17th century.

Bridge Street - Beyond the auction market site, the narrow bridge is probably late medieval while to the right the church of St Peter (5) was rebuilt in 1856-9 but stands on the site of a chapel built to offer prayers for the soul of Thomas a Becket's murderer. Most of the cottages and houses around the church originated in the 16th or 17th century and one was probably the church brewhouse. On the grass verge opposite stands the remains of another of Williton's old crosses.

In the direction of the Orchard Wyndham estate, the Orchard corn mill (6) stands on a gentle stream beyond the church, its waterwheel intact and its 18th century buildings now housing tearooms and a museum.

The dramatic former workhouse building in Williton awaiting redevelopment as modern housing.

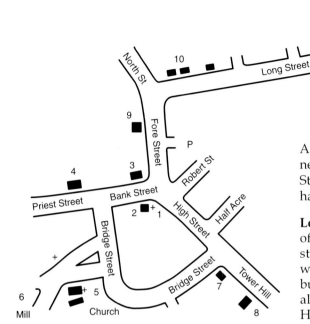

A market cross once stood near the corner with North Street one of three, or perhaps four, in the town.

Long Street - The north side of this aptly-named street starts with Nos. 1 and 3 which are both 17th century buildings with 20th century alterations. The White House Hotel (10), a former private house with headed carriage openings to the rear, is followed by the older Nos. 13 to 17 of 1624. Along this side of the road Nos. 29 and 45 are both of the 17th century but, like many such buildings, have been altered over the years. No. 33 was once a farmhouse. No. 51 is the interesting, and quite attractive former workhouse (11), built in 1838-40 by G.G. Scott and W. Moffat for the Williton Poor Law Union but later a hospital. With an impressive Bath stone entrance the building is laid out to a cruciform plan with octagonal centre.

On the other side Nos. 58 and 60 have medieval origins. Later a farm and barn they are now two cottages. No. 28 was a farmhouse of the same period.

Tower Hill / High Street - Where Bridge Street joins the main road note Toll Cottage (7) on the right hand corner. Beyond it lies the 1883 Methodist church (8).

Heading back towards the roundabout Half Acre on the right offers a 1724 terrace Nos. 4 to 8 and, from the previous century, Nos. 10 and 12, No. 14 and No. 33 The Forge. Also on the right is Robert Street where No. 3 is 16th century and Nos. 12-18 were a 17th century farmhouse.

Fore Street - This is the heart of Williton busy with traffic and shops, giving access to the library and council offices and containing the interesting Lloyds Bank building (9) with its ornamental dormers.

WINCANTON

HISTORY

Wincanton lies on a rising site by the modest River Cale and is well known for its milk industry, a major haulage and distribution company which bears its name and the National Hunt meetings which take place on the racecourse up Old Hill. The town may have Roman origins and was probably a Saxon settlement, but little is known of its history prior to the Norman Conquest. However, by the 12th century there was a significant agriculture-based presence by the side of the river and this steadily grew into a quasi-borough.

Like many of its neighbours, Wincanton grew prosperous as a cloth industry centre in the 15th and 16th centuries and long upper windows in some of the older surviving cottages bear witness to these links with the weaving industry. The dreadful plague which struck in 1552-3 was a serious setback to Wincanton's development but the town received a charter for an annual fair and regular markets in 1556 and this speeded the process of recovery.

In 1688 William of Orange stayed in Wincanton on his way to London and the first fighting with James II's troops took place nearby. Wincanton reaped a large dividend from its strategic position on the main road from London to Exeter and at one period as many as seventeen coaches a day stopped there for refreshments or fresh horses, duly provided by old inns like the White Horse and the Greyhound.

The 18th century began with a serious fire and then a smallpox outbreak but Wincanton started producing a

The view down Wincanton's High Street on the approach to the town from the north.

74

delft pottery about 1726, introduced by Nathaniel Ireson who set up house in the town at this time and went on to design many of the other notable houses in the area. The town also accommodated French prisoners from the Napoleonic wars and became a Poor Law Union centre in 1836. By this time the cloth industry was moving north but the arrival of the Dorset Central Railway in 1862 heralded a diversification of industry and activity that remains to this day.

THE WALK

From the car park in Carrington Way go up High Street as far as the junction with Ireson Road and Common Road, exploring both for a little way. Return along the south side and turn left to explore South Street and Tout Hill. Back to the Market Place, turn left down Church Street, right into Silver Street and right again, via Mill Street and High Street, to regain the starting point.

GAZETTEER

High Street - Among the assortment of 17th and 18th century buildings is No.51, a thatched public house dating from 1861 (1) and, just up Ireson Lane, the house (2) Nathaniel Ireson built for himself when he arrived in Wincanton in 1726. From here he managed the nearby pottery and helped to rebuild the town after the great fire.

On the other side of High Street there is a former tollhouse (3) of the

Wincanton Trust and dating from 1791 while back down the main road stands the Dolphin Inn (4), built by Ireson and known as the Rainbow Inn from 1774 to 1994. A variety of Georgian and other houses follow the ugly old hospital at the rear of No. 26 and at the bottom the 1733 White Horse Hotel (5) is an Ireson building that replaced a 1655 inn. Behind this is the site where the famous Cow & Gate brand of milk products originated.

Common Road - In addition to the tollhouse on the corner Balsam House (6), a little way down, is a delightful 17th century ensemble of Jacobean-style gables and windows.

South Street - Well worth scrutiny are No. 12 of 1836, No. 4 which is a former flax weaver's cottage from the 18th century, the 19th century Nag Inn and the typical pre-war cinema building.

Tout Hill - On the west side stands an impressive house formerly known as The Dogs (7) and once the stopover point for William of Orange. It was built by local merchant Richard Churchey around 1650 and altered by Ireson a century later. Companion cottages are nearly as venerable. The complex on the opposite side of the road (8) includes the c1795 Tout Hill House, now a convent school, the Roman Catholic Church of St Luke & St Teresa and the gaunt, multi-storey building of the Carmelite Fathers' Priory.

Market Place - A terrible fire raged through this area at the heart of Wincanton in 1707 but the lost buildings were steadily replaced by today's Georgian and Victorian houses, shops and inns. The first town hall was then wrecked by a mob in 1767 and its replacement burned down in another disaster 110 years later. The present corner building (9) dates from 1878 and is by W.J. Willcox. Nearby are three more ex-coaching era inns, the 1720 Bear, the c1743 Greyhound Hotel - once visited by Queen Victoria but now apartments - and the Red Lion of 1794 or earlier. The attractive Post Office (10) began life about 1796 and was formerly an inn.

Church Street - Varied and interesting, the street includes the Masonic Hall, once a silk factory, No. 7 which has its origins in the 15th century and has a medieval hall and No. 10 with an unusual, but very pleasant gabled frontage. The church of St Peter & St Paul (11) probably stands on a Saxon site at the riverside heart of the original settlement. A successor is known to have existed in 1344 but was altered in the 18th century and rebuilt, by J.D. Sedding, in 1887-91. There is a monument to Nathaniel Ireson, designed by himself, in the churchyard.

Mill Street - Probably the oldest street in Wincanton and once full of tiny shops, Mill Street has a very *period* atmosphere. The cottages are

mainly 18th century although Nos. 17 and 19 are possibly 200 years older. It also has the 1836-7 George Inn, the 1859 Congregational Chapel and school and the 1857 Baptist Chapel and school (12).

Also of interest are Sudden Grange (up West Hill) whose estate dates back to 1227, Bellfields in Southgate Road and probably the site of a bell foundry, and Dial House in The Batch, a 1690 building refronted in the 18th century. The complex of shops, library, information and other services in Carrington Way exemplifies the modern face of Wincanton.

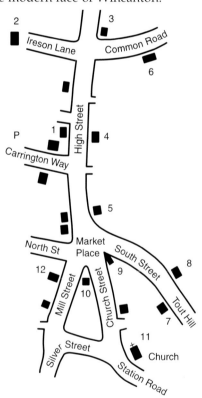

WIVELISCOMBE

HISTORY

Wiveliscombe lies among the southern slopes of the Brendon Hills and on the winding main road from Taunton to the Taw Estuary in Devon. Another important and very scenic route leads north through the hills to the former port of Watchet on the shores of Bridgwater Bay. Until 1966 Wiveliscombe also had a station on the former Great Western branch line to Barnstaple but it has always been an essentially rural town, important to the delightful area around, welcoming visitors but largely self-sufficient in its facilities and services. It is a varied, curious and pleasant place which holds much of interest for the explorer of Somerset by-ways.

There seems to have been both a Roman and a Saxon presence in and around Wiveliscombe but these origins were essentially pastoral. Prior to the Conquest the area, like many other vast tracts of land in Somerset, belonged to Edward the Confessor and he gave it to the Bishops of Bath and Wells who had some sort of manorial establishment at Wiveliscombe at the time of Domesday. To conduct church business in this part of the county the bishop then established new premises and a household in the town around the year 1256. By that time Wiveliscombe had a well-established church and a mill plus the beginnings of a domestic woollen industry that was to continue central to the town's existence for many years ahead.

Wiveliscombe gained further importance in 1285 when Edward I granted the bishop the right to hold a weekly market and a 3-day annual fair. The town became an established borough and had a number of shops which helped to supply the needs of the ecclesiastical establishment. Retailing remained important and by the 16th century the town had stalls, shambles and a market house as well as a small prison for those incapable of dealing honestly. Throughout the whole of this period the woollen industry had remained the mainstay of the town's activity with the production ranging from blanketing to the cloth that went via London to the West Indies to make up the 6-yard entitlement given annually to the slave population.

Wiveliscombe still has a number of 17th century buildings but the big changes in the town came in the 19th century, starting with the building of the Golden Hill Brewery on the hill in 1807. Following expansion of the Congregational presence in 1825, architect Richard Carver led the rebuilding of the crumbling medieval church in 1827-9. By this time the population figure was over 3,000 with 603 inhabited houses, 55% of the population engaged in agriculture and ten inns to supply their refreshment needs. The town hall was built in 1841-2 with the police station, banks, schools and library all coming along before the end of the century. The result today is a pleasant, well-located and well-provided little town with lots of local facilities, from swimming pool to popular community centre.

THE WALK

From the car park in North Street head for The Square and follow it left to explore Silver Street. Return and turn left along High Street and into Church Street. Pass round the church and back to Rotton Row, then left and right to South Street. Return along High Street, explore West Street and return to the car park.

GAZETTEER

North Street - Opposite and just beyond the car park is the ornate 1858 police station (1), now three houses. The primary school stands a little further on.

The Square - Between North Street and Silver Street a group of 3-storey bank etc buildings is followed by a delightful jettied building (2) decorated with abundant and ornate carvings. Known as the Court House the building dates from 1881 and houses the town library. On the opposite side of the square, full of civic pride, is the 1841-2 Town Hall (3) with clock and bell tower above and shops below.

Silver Street - On the right No. 2a, once a Roman Catholic chapel, is followed by No. 2, The Old Inn (4). On

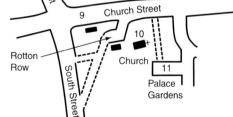

78

the opposite side the Court House group is followed by two Evangelical Congregational Church buildings (5). The present structures date from 1825 but the Noncomformist activity in Wiveliscombe goes back at least to 1708. No. 10 of 1887 was formerly the Parish Council Room.

High Street - This street was at the heart of the medieval town and offers a varied and intriguing mixture, with various interesting passages and courtyards leading off the main thoroughfare. The once-impressive block on the right (6) is early 19th century and the double 2-storey block opposite has a date of 1804 above the alleyway entrance. Parts of No. 14 are considerably older. On the left hand side there is a further mixture including No. 5 which was built around 1700 and the evocative archway between No. 8 and 9 (7) which may have led to the outer area of the summer palace of the Bishops of Wells.

Church Street - On the left, north side No. 25 (8), East and West Braynes, has 16th century origins while No. 27 is 17th century. On the right note No. 4 with its archway entrance and the Nos. 10 to 14 group (9) which are timber-framed and still display medieval bricks.

The Church - The angular, red sandstone church of St Andrews (10) was built in 1827-9 to the designs of Richard Carver and replaced an ailing medieval predecessor which, despite

At the heart of Wiveliscombe is The Square which is surrounded by interesting 19th century buildings.

its crumbling condition, needed gunpowder to bring it down. During the war some of the Anglican church treasures were stored in the vaults for safety.

The cross in front of the church is 14th century and while the church house/school along Rotton Row only dates from 1810 it incorporates much earlier fragments of ecclesiastical stonework. Beyond the churchyard in Palace Gardens is the main area of the former Bishop's Palace where an old archway (11) from that period survives.

West Street - The buildings here are mainly 19th century, starting with the substantial 4-storey block of No. 1 and the White Hart Hotel (12) opposite. On the left Wiveliscombe Jubilee Gardens (13) stand between The Croft and the pleasant 1930s-style garage building.

THE INFORMATION EXPERTS!

Tourist Information Centres can provide information, help and advice on a huge range of topics - accommodation, things to see and do, local services and facilities.... plus much more!
Take advantage of this valuable FREE store of expertise and contact the friendly staff at any of the centres listed here:-

Networked TIC's (affiliated to the Regional Tourist Board)

**Non-Networked Information Centres
(may be run by volunteers and may not operate accommodation booking services)**

**Exmoor National Park Visitor Centres
(not networked, do not operate accommodation booking services)**

Why not start your visit at the
SOMERSET VISITOR CENTRE on
the M5 at Sedgemoor Services
(between exits 21 & 22). The friendly
staff have information and advice for
the whole of Somerset -
Tel: **01934 750833**

BATH
Abbey Chambers
Abbey Churchyard, Bath.
Tel: 01225 477101
Email: tourism@bathnes.gov.uk

BRIDGWATER
50 High Street, Bridgwater.
Tel: 01278 427652
Fax: 01278 453489
Email: bridgwater.tic@sedgemoor.gov.uk

BURNHAM-ON-SEA
South Esplanade, Burnham-on-Sea.
Tel: 01278 787852
Fax: 01278 781282
Email: burnham.tic@sedgemoor.gov.uk

CHARD
The Guildhall, Fore Street, Chard.
Tel: 01460 67463

CHEDDAR
(in the winter months,
only open on Sundays)
The Gorge, Cheddar.
Tel: 01934 744071
Fax: 01934 744614
Email: cheddar.tic@sedgemoor.gov.uk

FROME
The Round Tower,
2 Bridge Street, Frome.
Tel: 01373 467271
Fax: 01373 451733
Email: frome.tic@ukonline.co.uk

GLASTONBURY
The Tribunal, 9 High Street,
Glastonbury.
Tel: 01458 832954
Fax: 01458 832949
Email: glastonbury.tic@ukonline.co.uk

GORDANO
Welcome Break Services,
M5, J19, Portbury.
Tel: 01275 375516 / Fax: 01275 373211

MINEHEAD
17 Friday Street, Minehead.
Tel: 01643 702624 / Fax: 01643 707166
Email: mineheadtic@visit.org.uk

PODIMORE VISITOR CENTRE
(only open April to end October)
The Travel Lodge Site, Podimore
Roundabout, A303, Nr Yeovil.
Tel: 01935 841302 / 01935 841294
Email: podimore.tic@southsomerset.gov.uk

SHEPTON MALLET
Tel: 01749 345258
Email: sheptonmallet.tic@ukonline.co.uk

SOMERSET VISITOR CENTRE
(closed Sat & Sun in the winter months)
Sedgemoor Services,
M5 South, Axbridge.
Tel: 01934 750833 / Fax: 01934 750755
Email: sominfo@msn.com

TAUNTON
The Library, Paul Street, Taunton.
Tel: 01823 336344 / Fax: 01823 340308
Email: tautic@somerset.gov.uk

WELLINGTON
30 Fore Street, Wellington.
Tel: 01823 663379 / Fax: 01823 663379
Email: welli1@globalnet.co.uk

WELLS
Town Hall, Market Place, Wells.
Tel: 01749 672552 / Fax: 01749 670869
Email: wells.tic@ukonline.co.uk

WESTON-SUPER-MARE
Beach Lawns, Weston-super-Mare.
Tel: 01934 888800 / Fax: 01934 641741

YEOVIL
(closed Sat & Sun in the winter months)
Petters House, Petters Way, Yeovil.
Tel: 01935 471279 / Fax: 01935 434065
Email: yeovil.tic@southsomerset.gov.uk

EXMOOR VISITOR CENTRES
NB. These are not networked TIC's.
They do not operate accommodation
booking services.

DULVERTON - Tel: 01398 323841
Email: dulverton@exmoor-nationalpark.gov.uk

DUNSTER - Tel: 01643 821835

COUNTY GATE
(only open in the summer months)
Tel: 01598 741321

**Information and advice may
also be obtained from the following
Non-Networked Local Information
Centres.**

BRUTON
Tel/Fax: 01749 812851

CARTGATE - (Display Board)
Picnic/Rest Area, A303.

CASTLE CARY
Tel/Fax: 01963 351628

CLARKS VILLAGE, STREET
Tel: 01458 447384
Fax: 01458 447393

CREWKERNE
Tel: 01460 73441 / Fax: 01460 78790
Email: crewkernecommunity
office@southsomerset.gov.uk

ILMINSTER - Tel: 01460 57294

LANGPORT - Tel: 01458 253527

PORLOCK
Tel: 01643 863150
Fax: 01643 863014

QUANTOCK INFORMATION CENTRE
Tel: 01278 733642
Fax: 01278 732845

SOMERTON
Tel: 01458 274070
Fax: 01458 274069

WATCHET - The Esplanade.

WINCANTON
Tel: 01963 34063 / Fax: 01963 34555

BLACKDOWN HILLS INFORMATION AGENCIES
NB. These are not networked TIC's.
They do not operate accommodation
booking services.

CLAYHIDON
Welcome Centre
Tel: 01823 680280

BLAGDON HILL
Village shop / Post office

BUCKLAND ST MARY
Village shop / Post office

COMBE ST NICHOLAS
Village shop / Post office